Foreword	ix
Introduction	xi
Day 1	1
Day 2	4
Day 3	7
Day 4	10
Day 5	13
Day 6	16
Day 7	19
Day 8	22
Day 9	25
Day 10	28
Day 11	31
Day 12	34
Day 13	37
Day 14	40
Day 15	43
Day 16	46
Day 17	48
Day 18	51
Day 19	54
Day 20	57
Day 21	60
Day 22	63
Day 23	66
Day 24	69
Day 25	72
Day 26	75
Day 27	78

Day 28	81
Day 29	84
Day 30	87
Day 31	90
Day 32	93
Day 33	96
Day 34	99
Day 35	103
Day 36	106
Day 37	109
Day 38	112
Day 39	115
Day 40	118

Foreword

IT IS MY distinct pleasure to recommend Mr. Rob Kimble's book, *I Just Got Saved...Now What?* This book is not a theoretical approach to beginning the Christian life, but a practical guide for the new believer to begin his daily walk with Jesus. It consists of forty brief chapters that are meant to be read each morning and applied throughout the day to the life of a follower of Jesus. You will read this book more than the first forty days of your walk with Jesus. It will become your constant companion, guiding you each step along the way as you embark on an ever deepening walk with our Lord.

In fact, I would highly recommend this book to seasoned followers of Jesus, as well, for two reasons:

1) It is grounded in God's Word. Every chapter highlights a specific scripture that is germane to our living out our faith every day.
2) It is not written by a novice. The truth in this book was forged on the anvil of Mr. Kimble's personal experience and his extensive work helping those who have been incarcerated encounter Jesus and make a fresh start walking daily with our Lord.

As Mr. Kimble says in the first chapter of his book, which discusses Proverbs 3:5-6, "If we do not exercise our faith, we can lose it like a dormant muscle." I assure you that, if you live out what this book teaches, your spiritual muscles will be well exercised, and you will be prepared to live out the purpose for which our Lord created you and redeemed you."

Thank you,

Chuck McAlister
Author – Speaker
"Helping people encounter Jesus."

Introduction

"I Just Got Saved...Now What?"

> **Matthew 28:19, 20 (NKJV) - "Go therefore and make disciples of all the nations, baptizing them in the name of the Father and of the Son and of the Holy Spirit, "teaching them to observe all things that I have commanded you; and lo, I am with you always, even to the end of the age." Amen.**

THE PREMISE OF this book is that you have just made a life-changing decision to make Jesus Christ your Lord and Savior, or, you have just returned to Jesus from an unfortunate departure of walking outside of the will of God. Either way, you have made the most important decision of your life in accepting the grace of Jesus Christ!

The title of this book asks the question, "Now what?" The answer to that question has occupied the heart and fueled the passion of this ministry which God has given me. I have been obsessed with a desire to encourage men to recognize the abundant promises contained in the Word of God. Promises from God assuring us that He will provide for us, that He will protect us, and that He will fight for us, if only we will trust Him. I want men and women to put their faith into action and realize their assured blessings in this life, as well as the life to come.

MY HISTORY WITH CHURCH

I grew up in a home in which my parents became new believers while I was a young toddler. I am filled with memories of church sermons, Sunday school classes, church picnics, AWANA events, and many other wonderful church social events for fellowship with other believers. Church was a place that I enjoyed, but it was merely a once-a-week part of my life; I did not have the everyday personal relationship with Jesus in which I felt I could lean upon Him 24/7.

My experience is synonymous with many others who grew up in the churches of that period. My church did a great job of teaching people the Word of God, leading people to salvation, and building a foundation of faith, but it was not great at discipleship. I do not blame the church leaders for my sinful departure—it was absolutely my fault. I pursued money and my own abilities, as a substitute for God, to overcome the obstacles of life. I do, however, recognize the substantial lack of focus in discipleship building within the few churches that I had attended during my developmental years.

That lack of discipleship building was also missing within my home. Although I have great God-fearing parents, they were new Christians within a body of believers who thought salvation was the end game instead of just the beginning. Mom and dad made many great changes to their lives in accordance with the progress of their own walks with God, but we did not worship or pray together outside of church. Jesus was for Sunday or Wednesday evenings rather than for every moment of every day.

I was taught what was right and wrong, but I wasn't taught how to search for God's help to *do* what was right and to *resist* what was wrong. I was just expected to do right, and when I stumbled, I was left feeling ashamed and insufficient. The Bible became a rule book to me, a standard to which I could never satisfy. Over time I became overwhelmed with so much guilt that I loathed going to church. I left the church without realizing the voluminous blessings and promises of God occupying the pages of the Bible.

TEACHING THEM TO OBSERVE ALL THINGS

Thanks to my wonderful parents and the foundation that my churches had given me, I knew where to go to when my chosen life crashed around me. I grabbed the study Bible that my father had given me, and I starting reading it in a completely different way. I read the Bible with an expectation that inside this book, God had revealed the mysteries to achieving a joyful life. I had a sincere belief that He would speak wisdom to me.

The selected verses at the beginning of this chapter are the answer to the question contained in the title, "now what?" We are told to "observe **ALL** things" that Jesus commanded, not just one or two things. If we will read the Bible with great seriousness, we will discover that Jesus wants us to have a great life in this world. He communicates how to achieve victories over the sinful world. He tells us how to exercise the power given to us as children of God in order to overcome addictions, lust, fear, bitterness, greed, and many other things that Satan uses to destroy our lives and the lives of those around us.

Jesus gave the churches their mandate in these verses as well—**"make disciples** of all nation." We, as Christians, are to lead others as a part of our own walk as disciples of Jesus. We are to follow His instructions on how to live in all aspects of our lives. Discipleship is not a one-time event or a short-term endeavor; discipleship is for the rest of our time on earth. Discipleship is not a religious event or ceremony, but rather it occupies our complete being. We should always be striving to become more like Jesus Christ.

I am continuously astonished as I recognize each day how God works in my life fulfilling the promises that He made in scripture. I have metaphorically walked through the parted Red Sea on numerous occasions as God has miraculously answered desperate prayers. I have stood upon specific promises of blessings and seen them to fruition on more occasions than I can remember. I have fought off depression, doubt, and other negative forces through the lens of the truth in the Word of God. I have been blessed with an ever-increasing faith each time I acknowledged God's actions in my life.

PURPOSE OF THIS BOOK

The purpose of this book is to help you during your beginning days after submitting your life to our Lord Jesus. Your church or ministry, in conjunction with Discipleship Ranch Ministries, has given you this book to help you navigate the Bible in order to realize many wonderful promises that God has made to you. These verses were so inspiring for my own walk with God, and many of them have dramatically altered the way I view life and the world around me.

You are also at the threshold of a time of trial in your life; the enemy will test your newfound faith in an attempt to thwart your ability to inherit the promised blessings of God. It is widely known that numbers in the Bible have significant meaning, and the number forty is universally recognized with its association of trials, probation, and testing. Dr. Ed F. Vallowe catalogs eight examples of the number forty (40) in periods of testing in his book *Biblical Mathematics: Keys to Scripture Numerics:*

1) Moses was in the mountain of Sinai forty days and nights receiving the Law. (Exodus 24:18)
2) This led to the making of the golden calf of Exodus 32:2-7. Thus, Israel fell under this forty days of testing. (Deuteronomy 9:18, 25)
3) After this they were tried forty years in the wilderness. (Numbers 14:34)
4) Forty days Elijah spent in Horeb after his experience on Mt. Carmel. (1 Kings19:8)

5) Forty days Jonah preached judgment would come to the city of Ninevah. (Jonah 3:4)
6) Forty days Ezekiel laid on his right side to symbolize the forty years of Judah's transgression. (Ezekiel 4:6)
7) Our Savior was tempted 40 days and nights of the Devil. (Luke 4:1-2)
8) Forty days Jesus was seen of His disciples, speaking of the things pertaining to the Kingdom of God. (Acts 1:3)

The forty brief chapters of this book are meant to be read at the beginning of each day. You will be introduced to a new verse or two each day, accompanied by a brief commentary introducing implications contained within them. You will be challenged to consider the Word of God in the context of your own life. You will be encouraged to pray for the fulfillment of those verses in you and your walk with God. You should also expect to hear the Holy Spirit reminding you throughout the day of what you have read earlier.

My prayer is that you will be inspired and encouraged in your walk so as to fully obtain the "exceeding great and precious promises" (2 Peter 1:4) God grants to those who love and follow Him. I am praying for you to experience the presence of God in your life.

Day 1

Proverbs 3:5, 6 - Trust in the LORD with all thine heart; and lean not unto thine own understanding.

In all thy ways acknowledge Him, and He shall direct thy paths.

I START THIS journey with you with the verses above because they have collectively become my "life verse." A life verse is a scripture that is very personal to your own walk with God and seems to have been written specifically for you. Proverbs 3:5, 6 are the very definition of a life verse for me.

When I came back to God after nearly fifteen years of running and hiding from Him, I remember falling on my knees to the ground in complete capitulation. I was exhausted from my efforts of trying to deal with the sinful consequences of my life which seemed to have mushroomed out of control in every facet: business, personal, physical, mental, and social. It was a therapeutic moment for me as God liberated me from the obligation to solve the numerous and immense problems in my life. I had finally succumbed to the realization that I needed more than just His help ... *I needed Him!*

Afterwards, I remember sitting on my bed with a Thomas Nelson NKJV Study Bible, which my father had purchased for me, and with a broken spirit I lifted my head up towards heaven saying, "Okay, God, I'm going to read this Bible to truly hear what You have to say to me." I opened the Bible and read it anew. It was no longer a book of stories of great men and events of the past, nor was it a book of dos and don'ts, it was the Word of God written for my benefit and understanding. I was reading what God had been wanting me to know all these years.

A NEW PHILOSOPHY

The verses above start off with, "Trust in the Lord with all your heart; and lean not on your own understanding." The definition of trust which I came to understand is—faith in action. Trust is a verb which requires doing something. If we do not exercise our faith, we can lose it, like a dormant muscle (2 Timothy 4:7; James 2:17). In this verse we are called to put our unwavering and complete faith in God's will for our well-being. That describes what I unwittingly did when I was on my knees. I surrendered all of my own will and abilities, and I sought God's will and divine abilities for my life.

As with every occasion in which God's heart is revealed to us, we see His mercy and grace promised to us along with His instruction. "In all thy ways acknowledge Him, and He shall direct your paths." This is a promise from God that if we will submit to His will for our lives, He will direct our every step. I am enamored with that promise and the significance of what it means to me. His assurance to me that He will direct my decisions in life literally keeps me from fearing anything that life throws at me. I know that God is in control so long as I do not take the wheel back from Him. This vow from Almighty God, the Creator of the universe, is life-changing to those that yield to it. Will you choose now to yield to it?

Before you say that you have already accomplished this, notice the detail of the instruction—"In **all thy ways** acknowledge

Him." We are required to give God control over all of our lives. This means your work, your hobbies, your marriage, your finances, your time, your family and everything in between. You cannot withhold any area of your life and expect to fool God into pouring the fullness of His promised blessings into your life. Simply put, this tells us to surrender all to Him. We must acknowledge that God has a role in every part of our lives; even more, He has full control over it.

I hope you will pray upon these verses and ask God to take control over your life. Remember, it doesn't require any skill on your part. All it takes is the decision and act of releasing the control and direction of your life to God ("lean not on your own understanding"). Yield yourself before our loving God, and let Him move you in the direction that He wants for your life. Ask God to help you trust in Him and to help you see His blessings along the way. Finally, remember to always "acknowledge Him" with prayers of thanksgiving.

Day 2

John 10:10 - The thief cometh not, but for to steal, and to kill, and to destroy: I am come that they might have life, and that they might have it more abundantly.

I WANT TO congratulate you on making it to Day 2. There is a famous quote by the Chinese philosopher Lao Tzu, "The journey of a thousand miles begins with a single step." I have realized that if I will turn my focus to the next step instead of the magnitude of the task in front of me, I soon find that I am well on my way to accomplishing what I set out to do.

I have a great affection for the verse above because it brought great clarity to the world around me. This verse summarizes the spiritual battle between Satan and Jesus, while disclosing our role as the focus of that battle. Satan is the "thief" in this verse, and his purpose is "to steal, and to kill, and to destroy."

A TIME OF RECOLLECTION

I felt that truth slap me across the face when I read this verse. As I reminisced about my past life, I saw that Satan had indeed tried to do all three of those terrible actions to me, and he had succeeded in two of them. He had stolen fifteen years from me, and he had destroyed all my good relationships, my career, my character, and any other good thing in my life. He also tried to kill me in many ways—addictions, depression, anger, etc.

The addictions that I took up were stealing my finances, destroying my relationships with those who loved me, and they were surely killing me physically. The resulting negative emotions and mindset kept me from making the proper decisions to change the course of my life. Satan kept me mired in an insurmountable hole which I kept digging deeper for myself. I was progressively settling for less and less in my life by seeking elusive moments of temporary happiness.

A PROMISE FROM OUR SAVIOR

After revealing the true intentions behind the destructive vices and pleasures of Satan's world, Jesus tells us why He came, "I am come that they might have life." Jesus came to die on the Cross for our sins so that we may have eternal life with Him and the Father. We all have earned death because of our sin (Romans 6:23), but Jesus paid that price for us. We have been given eternal life through the sacrifice of Jesus on the Cross (John 3:16)!

But Jesus was talking about more than just our spiritual afterlife; He was also talking about our lives here and now. Jesus came to give us life in this world, and not just a mediocre run-of-the mill life, but "life more abundantly." Jesus is promising each and every one of us an abundant life if we will yield to Him.

When I realized the meaning of this verse, I made a conscious decision to stand upon that promise by Jesus. As I look back, I can enthusiastically proclaim that He did exactly what He promised to me. I have an abundant life as a husband to my loving wife, an abundant life as a father of two precious daughters, an abundant life of a fulfilling prison and jail ministry, and an abundant life of friendships and church family. God has been so gracious to me in fulfilling that promise, and He will do so for you too.

All those blessings were at the end of a path in life which I never would have traveled on my own accord. I arrived there only by following the will of God in my life. Are you in need of life more abundantly? Do you believe that God knows how to give you life more abundantly? Will you trust Him?

I encourage you to look into your own life to see how the enemy has been stealing, killing, and destroying. Pray for God to give you discernment into the truths within your own life, and ask Him to help you trust in His ways. Stand upon the promises of Jesus in John 10:10 and call upon Him to make the changes in your life.

Day 3

Lamentations 3:22, 23 - It is of the LORD'S mercies that we are not consumed, because his compassions fail not.

They are new every morning: great is thy faithfulness.

DAY 3 WILL be a welcomed relief, like a cool drink at the end of a long desert walk. Today's verses reveal an incredible attribute about God's love for us that we may miss if we read them with the casualness of everyday life. Take a moment now to pause and intentionally ask God to reveal Himself to you in these verses.

I need to give thanks to K-LOVE, the Christian radio station, for my personal discovery of this verse. I was driving around town doing my daily runs of mail and bank deposits for work when I heard a brief segment in between songs designed to encourage the faith of the listeners. The speaker mentioned that God's Word says that, "His mercies renew every morning."

HIS MERCIES NEVER END

What an incredible proclamation contained within these two verses! God is revealing the nature of His love for us which is not manifested apart from Him.

- God's love for us is steadfast or resolute.
- His love never ceases for us.
- His mercies never come to an end for us.
- His mercies are new every single morning.

I genuinely needed to read that. I was in awe as I pondered the implications of what I just read. Although we often exhaust our love and affections for each other based on the circumstances in our relationships, God's love for us cannot be depleted in the least. No matter how much I mess up, His love for me will not diminish.

AN ATTACK OF THE ENEMY

A few days later, I was again driving around town doing the same work errands when something noteworthy happened. I was driving up to a mailbox in a parking lot where another car was driving precariously through the unused parking spaces in the wrong direction at a high rate of speed. I was forced to slam on the brakes to avoid a collision, and I instinctively lifted my hands palms up in a way to communicate to him, "What is your problem?" He, in turn, communicated his two middle fingers in response.

My anger was sparked, and I reacted negatively. I threw the gear into park and hurled open the door in a foolish endeavor to teach him a lesson. Fortunately, the man drove off without an incident. I returned to my car and continued with my tasks. As I was driving away, I began to review what just happened. My failed self-control was ever present before me.

Suddenly, I contemplated the possibility that this man might possibly show up at one of the Bible studies that I was beginning to teach. What would he think about the God that I would be teaching about when he saw me? How awful did I represent

God in my actions? My failure to maintain control produced an incredible amount of shame within me.

Then, the enemy started speaking to me, "What kind of Christian are you? You are a teacher of the Bible, and you act like that? God is so disappointed in you, and you are not worthy of teaching the Bible. You continue to fail, you hypocrite!"

VICTORY ACHIEVED

I was drowning in the pool of humiliation and guilt when I recalled reading Lamentations 3:22, 23. I spoke the verses out loud, "God's mercies renew every morning!" I shouted to Satan, "You are a liar! God is not finished with me; He loves me!" I repented to God for my actions, and my joy and peace were immediately restored. I felt so victorious over the lies that Satan was telling me, and he left defeated.

Have you ever had a similar experience where Satan tried to convince you that God doesn't love you anymore? Have you felt that you are not worthy of His love? Lamentations 3:22, 23 tell us that those feelings do not come from God, because His love for us is endless. Celebrate this truth by praying a prayer of thanks to God that you cannot do anything to stop Him from loving you. Engrave this verse into your heart so you can never be deceived about God's renewing love for you. God's mercies for you renew every day!

Day 4

1 John 5:14, 15 - And this is the confidence that we have in Him, that, if we ask any thing according to His will, He heareth us:

And if we know that He hears us, whatsoever we ask, we know that we have the petitions that we desired of Him.

I'M CONFIDENT THAT you will be rewarded for your commitment to this book with this next selection of verses. I have prayed at this very moment for each reader to be encouraged by the awesome promises of God and for His amazing powers to heal and bless your life and relationships.

The verses above reoccur throughout many of my Bible studies because of the incredible nature of what they proclaim. These verses actually promise you and me that if we ask God for anything within His will, He has to grant it! No question about it!

THE QUALIFIER…

The previous verse (1 John 5:13) sets up the qualifier for the promises contained in these verses. It says that we must believe in the name of the Son of God. If we believe in the name of Jesus, then He wants us to know that if we ask for anything "according to His will" that He absolutely hears the request. It does not fall on deaf ears, nor does it get lost in the masses of prayers from everyone else. God hears it!

The verses go on to say that since we know that He hears our prayers, "We know that we **have the petitions** that we desired of Him." God just promised us that He will fulfill the prayer request that we just asked of Him. That is incredible power given to us as children of God, and this should have a significant change in our state of mind. We can quit worrying about so many things that weigh so heavily on most other people because God has promised you and me that He would grant those petitions.

EXAMPLES OF GOD'S WILL

As with many men, I have worried about my ability to provide a living for my family. I need not worry about this anymore because Genesis 2:15 informs us that men were created to work. Since I know that it is God's will for me to work, I can then know if I ask God to fulfill a need of a job, He will provide one. This realization has produced a tremendous amount of peace for me as a man, husband, father and a provider.

Are you dealing with an addiction that seems to be beyond your own ability to quit? Galatians 5:1 and Romans 8:15 reveal that it is God's will for us to be free of any bondage, which is what an addiction becomes to us. If so, pray with confidence for God to free you from the control of the addiction. Quit trying to do this on your own and ask God right now to free you from drugs, alcohol, nicotine, or whatever else has an unhealthy control over you.

Have you been suffering through loneliness? Genesis 2:18 tells us that God did not create us to be alone. Pray to God with absolute confidence for Him to provide you with the husband/wife He has created for you.

Are you overwhelmed with bitterness for another person because of the pain they have caused you? It is God's will for us to be free of the cancerous effects of harboring bitterness toward others (Matthew 18:21, 22). Pray with certainty that God will remove the hate and pain from you.

Is your marriage in jeopardy? Does it seem like you are in a hopeless situation without any clue of how to fix it? We can pray to God knowing that it is God's will for us to be "one flesh" with our spouses (Matthew 19:5; Genesis 2:24). I had six months of desperate prayers for God to save my marriage, and now I'm enjoying the fruits of those prayers.

Finally, there are so many unknown details about God's specific will for your life which we cannot deduce from the Bible, but God will reveal this to you through prayer and thought. Trust Him, and pray for His will to flourish within all areas of your life. Seek God's will for you each and every day. Keep today's verses close to your heart so you can quickly vanquish the seeds of doubt which chokes out our faith.

Day 5

Ephesians 3:20 - Now unto Him that is able to do exceeding abundantly above all that we ask or think, according to the power that worketh in us.

I HOPE YOU were encouraged and comforted by yesterday's revelation of the absolute certainty of receiving our prayer requests when we ask for God's will in our lives. Today, God will greatly expand our expectations for the many other appeals that we pray to Him for.

Within most churches, there is a group of people that will serve the body of believers as a prayer team. The prayer team member will incur occasions where people come with a desperate plea such as healing from cancer or a brain tumor. In moments like these, the prayer team member naturally feels a conflict between a desire for that person's petition to be granted and the angst of the improbability of the request happening under normal circumstances. A common response to these opposing forces is to issue a get out of a miracle free card to God by inserting a conditional "if it is in Your will" in the prayer request.

GOD'S EXPECTATION TO US

When we read the verse above very carefully, we see that God is informing us that we should pray in a manner that is far above what we think is possible. He tells us that He is capable to, "Do exceeding abundantly above all that we ask or think." God is still in the miracle business, and He wants us to faithfully bring these miracle type requests to Him.

There are plenty of examples of miracles in the Bible, but to me, the parting of the Red Sea to allow the Israelites to escape the Egyptian army rises to the top. In my own life, I have walked through several metaphorical Red Seas as God answered my dire prayers. When we see God's hand influencing the circumstances around us, our faith gets increased exponentially. We get glimpses at God's incredible power, abilities, and love for us.

MIRACLES OBSERVED

Let me share an example of a miracle that I witnessed in someone with whom I prayed. I was teaching a weekly Bible study on the topic of the power of God in the local county jail, and I finished with an invitation to pray together for any needs. One distraught man responded about his sister's medical condition. He talked about an accident she was in and described that she was brain dead. The air of hope inside me vanished as I prayed with him for his sister's recovery.

My lack of faith bothered me all week, and it seemed like God was speaking to me for something specific. All week I contemplated my failure, and my Bible reading that week seemed to be tailored to the topic of praying in faith. On the morning prior to my return to the jail, I actually communicated to my mother about what had been bothering me all week. I ended with a determination that I would not pray with a get out of a miracle free attitude; rather, I would pray with an expectation that God would perform a miracle.

That evening I recall teaching a very inspirational Bible study. As I looked around the room, I could easily observe the group of men realizing the love of God for them. However, the man that I had prayed with last week spent the whole evening with a visible distressed look upon his face, and he would not make eye contact with me throughout the study. I knew he had not received the miracle that he was seeking.

God spoke to me during that lesson, and I kept the man from leaving afterwards by inquiring if he was upset about his sister. When he confirmed my belief, I asked him if we could pray again. This time, I felt a peace within me that God was going to do a miracle, and I voiced that in the prayer. We asked God to do a miracle healing of his sister.

I was so anxious for the week to pass with a building anticipation that I would hear great news about his sister. As the men filed into the multi-purpose room the following week, I watched with disappointment as the man was not included in the group. I identified one of the other men who had participated in our prayer the previous week to inquire about the missing man. He informed me that the man was transferred to a different cell block, but he also shared with me that the man's sister awoke from her coma and was not brain dead!

DO YOU NEED A MIRACLE

I am in need of reading this verse over and over again to reinforce my awareness of the fact that God is not burdened with our needs and troubles. God delights in giving good things to those who love Him. He delights in restoring family relationships that were thought to be beyond repair. He delights in providing provision where once there only stood hopelessness. God is the same miracle-working God today as He was back then.

It is my hope that you grasp the heart of God through this revelation. God has a desire for you to approach Him with the enormous problems in your life. Do not hesitate another minute if you are dealing with a heavy burden; rather be encouraged with Ephesians 3:20 and take that dilemma to God right now.

Day 6

Proverbs 16:3 (NKJV) - Commit your works to the LORD, And your thoughts will be established.

I'M CONFIDENT THAT you have experienced God's presence at some point during the past week of our discipleship journey through this book. The Bible reveals to us that God is speaking to us at all times (Job 33:14), but we do not hear Him if we are not endeavoring to listen for Him. Today's verse will help us recognize one way in which God speaks to us.

Ever since I surrendered my life completely to God, I have wanted to hear from God personally. Whenever I had an occasion to meet a new faith leader I would ask about how that person hears God. I was eager to experience the clarity of God speaking to me which so many other people had expressed experiencing at some point.

A PRAYER OF GOD'S WILL ANSWERED

Day 4 conveyed God's promises to grant our petitions of anything within God's will, and I can confirm that promise within my own life on numerous instances. I had been growing tremendously in godly wisdom through my studies, which was another answered prayer from Day 4, but I did not have a fruitful prayer life. I was faithful in the effort of praying, but I struggled mightily with it. I regularly found myself laboring with my words just to occupy the allotted time for prayer. My prayer morphed into an empty routine instead of the loving, encouraging, and peaceful dialogue with our Father in heaven that it should be.

Having experienced the faithfulness of God answering my previous prayers, I should have realized that I should just ask God to help me pray better. Once I did realize this, I immediately asked God to help me with my prayer life. I asked Him to help me be able to hear His will for me and to have a productive prayer life.

I don't recall how much time later, but it wasn't very long afterwards I was stumbling through another prayer when I heard (not audibly), "Stop talking and listen." I stopped speaking for the first time and just stayed in the spirit of prayer. It was awkward at first, but I soon noticed that my mind started thinking about a new study for the prison ministry. Verses for that study popped into my mind along with structure for that study. I realized that God had put those thoughts into my mind once I stopped to listen to Him!

Over time, I've learned to recognize the difference between my thoughts and His thoughts. I've also learned to have a dialogue with Him, to ask specific questions when I hear from Him. God has been so generous in granting my petition that I truly believe praying with others has changed from a personal weakness to a major strength within the ministries which God has given me.

COMMIT YOUR WORKS TO THE LORD

Soon after the experience described above, I stumbled over our Day 6 verse. I realized that I had committed my works to God in the act of asking to become better at praying. I was asking for a relationship with God, which is exactly what God wants from us (Acts 17:26, 27). I got so excited from understanding Proverbs 16:3 and recognizing that God did in fact establish my thoughts as promised in that verse. God speaks to me in many diverse ways, but in my prayer life, He establishes my thoughts.

I encourage you to approach God with a similar request in asking Him to help you hear from Him. Start your prayer in a spirit of esteem by being thankful for what He's done and praising Him for who He is. Quote Proverbs 16:3 to Him and request God to allow you to discern His thoughts. Praise Him, quote His Word, request His will, then stop talking and listen! It may take a while for you to discern when God is actually talking to you, but you will soon be able to look back with certainty knowing when it was Him.

Day 7

> 1 John 1:9 - If we confess our sins, He is faithful and just to forgive us our sins, and to cleanse us from all unrighteousness.

DR. CHUCK MISSLER of Koinonia House labels the verse above as the Christian's bar of soap. That phrase stuck with me because of the implication that all Christians will make mistakes requiring the need for a spiritual bath. Have you found yourself falling short of the standard of God this past week?

God's laws are impossible for us to keep on our own behalf, and we are told that there is not one of us that are righteous (Proverbs 14:3; 53:3; Romans 3:10, 12). It is God's will for us to stop sinning, but this will be a lifelong effort paved with some failures. The Holy Spirit's job description is to convict us of "sins, righteousness, and judgment" (John 16:7, 8) in an effort to correct us. We will experience His conviction on many occasions when we first start walking with God, and we should not feel that God is mad at us or finished with us. In actuality, God is teaching us like a loving parent corrects a child.

A SUCCESSFUL TRAP OF SATAN

Satan's purpose is to get us out of God's will so that we will be outside of God's protection and blessings. In order to get us out of God's will, Satan has to get us to doubt God's Word (Genesis 3:1). One of Satan's tactics is to shame us into giving up when we make a mistake. Satan tells us that, really, we are not saved and not worthy of God. He will try to put the whole burden of living righteously upon our own shoulders so that we collapse under the massive weight.

1 John 1:9 removes any doubt about God's unyielding love for us. It says that if we will admit our sins to Him, then God forgives us. It says that God is "faithful" to clean us from "all unrighteousness." We confess—God forgives everything—Satan is defeated! God's love is expressed in this verse by showing His desire for us to live without the cancerous guilt of sin. He wants us to stop sinning, but He does not throw us away when we do sin.

MY USE OF THE BAR OF SOAP

Just the other day, I was so convicted regarding God's instruction for us to honor each other. Listening to a sermon by Larry Stockstill, I was convicted by my own deficiencies in obeying this instruction that I prayed immediately for God's help in this. I saw how far I was from meeting God's standard set forth in the Bible, and I committed to change this with God's help.

Regrettably, I didn't even make it through the afternoon before I dishonored my sister. We had a celebration for her youngest son's graduation at my house, and I made a comment designed to convey my dislike for how she was dressed. I did not honor my sister (in the presence of our parents) within a few hours after I had committed to God to do so.

I felt the weight of my failure for the rest of the day. I attempted to rationalize what I had done, but the conviction remained. I was awakened in the middle of the night with the crescendo of weight from my sin. I immediately picked up the bar of soap and confessed my sin to God. I quoted this verse to God in an effort to thank Him for His promise to make me clean in His righteousness.

I was instantly comforted by God's love. I was assured by the promise in 1 John 1:9, and when I followed God's instruction, I experienced the faithfulness of God to forgive me. The peace of God's forgiveness yielded the sleep that the weight of my sin had disturbed.

Forgiveness is an amazing attribute of our God. We need to always remember that it is God's desire for us to come to Him for grace and forgiveness. He wants you to live apart from sin, but He will always be ready to forgive you when you don't.

Have you felt the burden of sin and failure? Has Satan ever tried to guilt you into giving up your walk with God? 1 John 1:9 is God's prescription to remedy our sins. You can absolutely be assured that God will be there every time to forgive you and cleanse you!

Day 8

John 8:31, 32 - Then said Jesus to those Jews which believed on Him, If ye continue in my word, then are ye my disciples indeed;

And ye shall know the truth, and the truth shall make you free.

JUST LIKE PROVERBS 3:5, 6 is my life verse (see Day 1), the verses above have become my ministry's "life verse." I have been given tremendous clarity in the correlation between a person's longevity of a healthy walk with God and their daily commitment to Bible reading. You cannot have one without the other.

I know without uncertainty that I have been rewarded by God in my pursuit of knowing His Word (Hebrews 11:6). God has blessed me with wisdom, understanding, and so much more. God has opened my eyes to view the world through the lens of His Truth, yielding a new understanding, new priorities, new paths, and a joyful life.

It happens gradually, similar to the sand falling in an hour glass. No individual truth will be recognized to be life-altering in itself, but the collection of revelations over time turns your life upside down. Soon you discover that you are completely different from the person who started the initial journey with God as He remakes you in the image of Jesus Christ (Romans 8:29).

A MISUNDERSTANDING REMEDIED

I have noticed that many people have misunderstood the verses above just as I once did. I had believed that the verses were admonishing us to tell the truth, and that the truth-telling would set us free from all the hazards and consequences of lying. This, however, is simply not what the scripture is teaching.

The verses open with the context of whom the following instruction will apply to, in this case, those "Jews which believed on Him." Jesus was talking to the believing Jews in contrast to the unbelieving Jews. In other words, He was talking to the followers of Jesus Christ, like you and me.

Next, Jesus gives the condition by which we must qualify in order to receive the promise. This condition is evident by the word "if." If you do this, then He will do that. Let's diligently look at the condition—"If you continue in my word." Jesus is telling the believers (think Christians) that if we will abide in His Word daily, then we are His disciples. Being disciples of Jesus will allow us to see the truth, and this truth that we can now see will set us free from all bondage.

TRUTH REVEALED

God was revealing His way to me, and I was experiencing an abundance of blessings for my obedience in following His way. My marriage was being healed rapidly. My addictions were overcome. My life became fulfilling in all its aspects, and I experienced the soothing peace of God wrapped around me like a warm blanket on a cold evening.

His truth has given me a completely different mindset and philosophy from that which I held before. I have found institutions which I once coveted and adored to be devious and unhealthy. I have shed strongly-held beliefs and ideals upon realizing that they were designed to encourage an independence in opposition to God. I was finding that my whole belief system was corrupted and spiritually anemic.

I have been active in numerous ministries representing all demographics and backgrounds, and I have observed a common factor among those who vocalize a real struggle in their spiritual life. When I ask how often they read their Bible, I get replies such as, "I don't have time to read" or "I know I should read the Bible, but..." The absence of a daily Bible reading will hinder your ability to know and act on the truths of God.

If you have been diligent in reading the Bible daily, then I encourage you to continue along with an expectation for God's truths to be revealed to you. If you have not, then I strongly urge you to make that commitment now. Pledge yourself to read a single chapter of the New Testament each morning. This will take no time at all. End each evening by reading a single chapter from Psalms or Proverbs, rotating between the two. Set aside a time between the two for reading a chapter of the Old Testament. Ask God to put a desire in your heart to study His Word. Take stock in your daily routine searching to eliminate something unhealthy or unprofitable and replacing it with His truth and wisdom.

Day 9

> 2 Timothy 3:16 - All scripture is given by inspiration of God, and is profitable for doctrine, for reproof, for correction, for instruction in righteousness:

I PROBABLY SHOULD have started our journey with this verse due to its importance on how we perceive the Bible. An accurate understanding of 2 Timothy 3:16 will increase exponentially the reverence we have for the Word of God.

The Greek word translated into "inspiration of God" above is *theopneustos*. *Pneu* meaning "to blow," which is where we get the word pneumonia from (pneumonia is a lung infection making it very difficult to breathe). The prefix *theo* means God. The literal translation being "God breathed." All scripture is God breathed!

AN INCORRECT PERCEPTION

I have been blessed with a desire to study God's Word, and in that pursuit, I have read numerous commentaries by many different authors. There are a number of commentaries that lose my attention almost immediately causing me to place the book back upon the shelf. This happens when the author attempts to tell the reader that we need to understand the history of the writer of the book of the Bible, or the culture of the time period of the writer, in order to understand that book of the Bible. This writer does not share the same esteem I have for what our verse today claims—which is that the Author of the entire Bible is God Himself!

It may be Paul's hand or John's hand writing the majority of the New Testament, but it was the Holy Spirit which gave them the words to write (2 Peter 1:20, 21; 2 Samuel 23:2; Luke 1:70; Acts 1:16). This is true for all sixty-six books that make up the Bible. God wrote Genesis 1 through Revelation 22, and everything in between.

AN ASSURANCE WITH A PURPOSE

In fact, the opening phrase we just analyzed is meant to assure the reader that the following four-fold purpose will be fulfilled specifically because it was God who wrote the Bible. The four-fold purpose is that all scripture is profitable...

for doctrine -	what is right
for correction -	what is wrong
for instruction -	how to get it right
for reproof -	how to stay right

Whenever you read the Bible, you can be assured that the principles and truths contained are applicable to you, right here, right now. God's truths are ageless and never need to be updated or adjusted (Hebrews 13:8). Although there is context in the Bible that we should strive to understand, the Word of God is alive and will speak to the very core of our souls (Hebrews 4:12).

With this in mind, let us not open the Bible with the casualness of a grocery magazine; but rather, let us read the Word with the deference that it deserves. We should read it with the knowledge that God breathed these words to us for our relief and benefit. We are reading a love letter from our spiritual Father with divine instructions on how to navigate successfully through life to a reunion with Him in eternity.

Take just a minute now to thank God for His Word, and ask Him to give you a desire to know and understand the Bible. Thank God for His love for you and seek to have Him speak to you daily through the Bible. Finally, expect His Word to reveal His instructions on how to do the things that are right and to avoid doing the things that are wrong. God's blessings will surely follow the men and women that commit to do His will.

Day 10

> Genesis 3:1 - Now the serpent was more subtil than any beast of the field which the LORD God had made. And he said unto the woman, Yea, hath God said, Ye shall not eat of every tree of the garden?

CONGRATULATIONS FOR REACHING the one-quarter mark of our forty-day journey through this book. Hopefully, you have experienced God in your life through the lens of the selected verses which we have covered already. I hope you are also increasingly discovering how to hear God speak to you directly through the Holy Spirit (1 Corinthians 2:14).

We are going to take a look today at a verse that had a profound effect in my own life. Upon understanding the immense truth camouflaged within the simplicity of the verse, I obtained an awareness of the core tactic that Satan uses on us all. This knowledge is fundamental to protecting ourselves from the "wiles of the devil" (Ephesians 6:11). We tend to focus our defensive efforts on addressing the symptoms and the reasons of the specific sins—such as drugs, alcohol, adultery, etc.—all the while overlooking the actual source of all sin in general.

THE PREFIX TO THE FIRST SIN

Genesis 3:1 tells us that Satan ("the serpent") is more subtle (cunning, wily, crafty, insidious, clever, etc.) than any other creature God created. We were given an adjective describing a very sneaky and devious quality of Satan. He is without equal in all of God's kingdom in being able to attack us without us realizing it.

The next part of the verse gives the reader a demonstration of Satan's craftiness. It says that Satan asked Eve, "Yea, hath God said...?" We find in that one little question, Satan asks Eve, the method he uses to lead the entire world into sinning—doubt. He put doubt into Eve's mind in regards to what God had said.

With doubt inserted into her mind, Eve goes on to misquote God by altering some detail and inserting other details. Finally, she succumbs to a lie that Satan gave her with an immeasurable consequence to the entire world, and all of this started with the initial doubt in God's Word.

THE BIG PICTURE

God created us to do His will and purpose, but He gave mankind a free will to choose for ourselves. When we obey God, we are within His will where we are protected and provided for. Satan's goal is to get us out of God's will where we become exposed and vulnerable. In order to get us out of God's will, he must first get us to doubt in God's Word.

Satan doesn't care which sin entraps us; he only cares that we are separated from God. He will then shackle us to an addiction of our choosing, hindering us from walking with God. All our sins arrive from an original doubt in the promises and instructions of God.

How easy is it for Satan to get us to doubt what God said when we are not reading God's Word? Very easy. In order to combat

Satan at the source, we must be vigilant in our Bible reading. Jesus attacked Satan's efforts to tempt Him by quoting scripture as a correction to what Satan was saying (Matthew 4; Luke 4). Jesus showed us how to defend ourselves against Satan's subtle but dangerous attacks on us—quote God's Word to him.

We are bombarded with the world's false wisdom and negativity all day long through people, social media, news, TV, schools, magazines, movies, etc. We need to dramatically decrease the consumption of the world's culture and attributes, and fill our minds with God's love, grace, and wisdom.

Take this moment to thank God for His love for you, and ask Him to instill a thirst to consume His Word. Make a standing appointment in your daily schedule to read the Bible. Build upon your daily prayer life by finding opportunities to thank Him for something. Instill daily habits of Bible reading and prayer, and then bask in the comfort and protection of God's provision for your life.

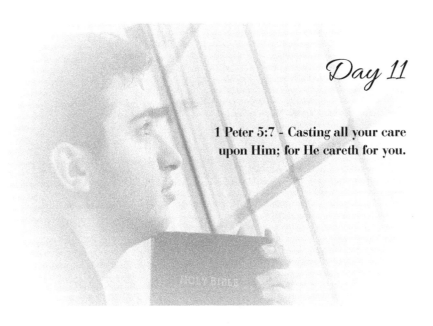

Day 11

1 Peter 5:7 - Casting all your care upon Him; for He careth for you.

YOU MAY RECOGNIZE this verse as the source of a popular song by the contemporary Christian band, Finding Favour, in their song *Cast My Cares*. Not too long ago, I selected this verse for our nightly family devotion as the memory verse for the week, and my wife immediately starting singing the song. The song, however, did not include the most important part of the verse above.

I intentionally listed 1 Peter 5:7 as the follow-up to Day 10 because I wanted to link these two together. In the Genesis 3:1 commentary, it was demonstrated that the core of Satan's method for getting people out of God's will begins with putting doubt in their minds about God's Word. There is a simple, but significant statement in this verse that Satan does not want us to believe—"for He careth for you."

We are told in this verse to put our cares upon God's shoulders because God cares for you and me. His care for you and me is the motive for us to trust that He will attend to our concerns for our well-being. Is there anyone else you would rather put in charge of your welfare? Is there anyone more capable of affecting better results? Is there anyone more affluent or prosperous? The answers to each of these questions are obviously "no."

TRUTH REPLACED WITH DOUBT

If we agree that there is no one more suitable and powerful to provide for our needs and cares than God, then what would make us lean upon our own selves instead of God? The only reason we would do such an incredibly absurd thing is if we didn't believe that God would act for us. Here lies Satan's subtle strategy for affecting our behavior. Satan injects doubt into our hearts and minds that God "careth for you."

We start to think that God is too busy to concern Himself with our daily troubles. We incorrectly assume that God will not help us because He is mad at us, or disappointed with us. We believe that unless we act for ourselves, we will not achieve our goals, or obtain the necessities of life. We erroneously limit God's help to the really important matters to the detriment of ourselves. We act foolishly and eventually succumb to the weight of the world upon our shoulders.

GOD'S UNCONDITIONAL LOVE

Our verse today tells us that we should bring all our concerns to God no matter how small they are because He loves and cares for us. Over and over again, the Bible reveals to us the extent of God's love. His love is a pure commitment of love from Him, and it requires no action or response from us. His love does not change, nor is His love conditional.

If we will acknowledge God's unconditional love for us, then we can defeat Satan's primary tactic for getting us to draw ourselves away from God. We should conquer Satan the same way that Jesus did—by quoting scripture. When Satan puts doubt in our minds about God's concern for us, we can say, "No, God cares for me."

I have fought this fight with Satan numerous times, and I have seen God respond faithfully and generously. I have observed God performing nothing short of miracles in my life; but, more importantly, I repeatedly see God answering the daily prayers of my life. I cannot imagine waking up without first coming to God for His daily provision and protection of my life.

Take this moment to thank God for His unconditional love for you. Thank Him for His willingness to take all your cares and concerns upon Himself. Then, take your daily concerns to God seeking His input and help. Finally, be watchful in anticipation of God acting on your behalf, for He cares for you!

Day 12

Philippians 4:6 - Be careful for nothing; but in every thing by prayer and supplication with thanksgiving let your requests be made known unto God.

WE DISSECTED 1 Peter 5:7 yesterday learning that God cares so much for you and me that He asks us to lay all of our troubles upon Him. Today, we are going to get instruction on how to do that.

The verse above opens with, "Be careful for nothing." The Greek word translated above to "careful" is *merimnao*, which means—to be anxious. We are told to be anxious for nothing. God does not want His sons and daughters to be filled with distress or apprehension about anything at all. God does not want us to be consumed with worry about deadlines, promotions, due dates, misfortunes, or any of the daily struggles that weigh upon us. God wants to relieve us of those burdens, thereby liberating us from all fear.

THE SUBSTITUTION

In contrast to worrying, we are commanded to pray. We are simply instructed to convert our burdens into prayers. Whenever we start to dwell on a problem or a forthcoming difficult decision, we should immediately bring them to God through prayer. We should ask Him for the result, ability, or decision that we are seeking.

In case you may feel hesitant about bothering God with the small or petty matters, the verse ends with, "Let your requests be made known to God." It is an invitation to us to make sure God hears our troubles. We are specifically directed to voice everything to Him.

Last year my family took a vacation to SeaWorld and Six Flags in San Antonio, Texas. A few weeks before we were scheduled to depart, I realized that I had completed all the scheduling and purchasing for the vacation without once going to God in prayer seeking His input. I immediately went to prayer with an apology to God for leaving Him out of the decision-making process, and I asked God to bless the vacation and to keep our family safe.

From the day before the start of vacation and continuing through the long drive to San Antonio, my wife was in much gloom over the weather forecast declaring one hundred percent chance of heavy rain for the week. The local government authorities were preparing for severe flooding all throughout southern Texas, and my wife was worried about the prospect of spending the entire week in a hotel room wasting away all our time, effort, and money. Upon arrival, I gathered our family on the hotel bed, and, holding hands in a prayer, we asked God to bless us with good weather. He did indeed answer our prayer by delaying the huge storm unto our rear view mirror as we were departing home! Our concern for good weather on our vacation was not too trivial for God to answer.

THE KEY INGREDIENT

Although I have long had a fondness for this verse, I had overlooked the key ingredient which we were instructed to include with our prayers—thankfulness. My pastor emphasized this detail one night during a prayer gathering, and I immediately heard the Holy Spirit corroborate the significance within me. We are repeatedly told throughout the Bible to be thankful in our prayers to God (Colossians 4:2; 1 Thessalonians 5:16-18).

Among the various prison and jail ministries which I am blessed to be a part of, I often create opportunities for everyone to pray together. In each of those occasions, we start by giving thanks to God for something in our lives. I always feel incredibly close to God during these moments of prayer. The Holy Spirit is ever present to us at those times, exchanging our frustrations and doubts for joy and peace.

Are you dealing with worries and anxiousness? Do you feel the weight of needs or decisions pressing upon you? Then indulge God on His desire to deal with your problems on your behalf. Start by being thankful to God for whatever situation you are currently in. Declare your trust in God to provide what is best for you. Voice your faith in God's ability to provide for your needs. Ask God to act on your behalf, believing that He will do as He has promised.

Day 13

Philippians 4:8 - Finally, brethren, whatsoever things are true, whatsoever things are honest, whatsoever things are just, whatsoever things are pure, whatsoever things are lovely, whatsoever things are of good report; if there be any virtue, and if there be any praise, think on these things.

TODAY'S VERSE IS quite lengthy and contains eight specific qualifications of topics that we should lend our minds to. I find this verse very relevant in our walk with God. The wisdom contained within this verse is worthy of the serious consideration we are going to exercise today.

I purchased an oval above-ground pool at the request of my wife for our two daughters. This purchase came with an obligation for me to perform daily maintenance in order to uphold the integrity of the water. One of the chores required is to change out the water filter no less than once every two days. After three days, the bright white fabric filter will emerge a dark slimy brown littered with dead insects. Without changing or cleaning the filter, it will soon circulate contaminated water into the swimming pool.

Our minds are similar to the water filter, and our hearts are the swimming pool. Our minds act as a filter of what we allow to enter our hearts. If we engage our minds to consume large amounts of impurities, then our hearts and subsequent actions will become impure as well.

THE THIRTY-DAY CHALLENGE

As far back as I can remember, I have always been a consumer of politics and world events. I read books on presidents, tell-all books from people within an administration, and books from generals that led war campaigns. My mornings consisted of a good hour perusing numerous websites containing news articles from around the world.

It was how I spent the rest of the days and evenings that finally revealed a dark effect upon me. I would listen to talk radio throughout the day and non-stop Fox News coverage throughout the evenings. These shows were completely founded upon two or more individuals with opposing views arguing at each other. Consuming ten plus hours per day of this left me a very angry person. I had to do something different.

I was never much of a music person in church, but I decided to substitute talk radio for K-LOVE. This transition affected me immediately. I found my tension fleeing and joy was filling the vacuum. K-LOVE markets a thirty-day challenge for the new listener to switch to worship music and invites him or her to evaluate the positive influence it has upon the listener's life. I noticed it intensely!

I made many other changes in my life for similar reasons. I turned off the senseless arguing on Fox News and replaced it with books and study materials. I also committed to only reading the Bible, books about the Bible, or books espousing life-improving skills. Throughout the years, I am constantly making adjustments into what movies I watch, or what TV shows I view.

GOD'S FILTER FOR US

Our verse today gives us eight specific filters—true, honest, just, pure, lovely, good report, virtue, or praise. What are you allowing into your mind? What are you consuming on Facebook, Instagram, Snapchat or any other social media? What does your internet search history declare about your web viewing? Would you categorize your media input as true, honest, just, pure, lovely, good report, virtue, or praise?

What are the typical subjects that occupy your conversations with friends? What are the books or magazines that interest you? Are you filling your mind with contaminants which will soon clog up your heart? Maybe it's time to change the filter. Take this moment to ask God to show you what pollutant is harming your heart. Then be obedient in laying that down and replacing it with something true, honest, just, pure, lovely, good report, virtue, or praise.

Day 14

> 2 Corinthians 11:3 - But I fear, lest by any means, as the serpent beguiled Eve through his subtilty, so your minds should be corrupted from the simplicity that is in Christ.

I WANT TO open this day by congratulating you for being diligent in reaching the end of the second week in this forty-day discipleship journey. I'm confident that you have heard from the Holy Spirit along the way, and I pray you have recognized God's involvement in your life.

Today's verse links us back to what we discussed in Day 10 (Genesis 3:1) about how Satan inserts doubt into our minds regarding God's Word. In this verse, Paul is concerned that the church of Corinth would be deceived by Satan just as Eve was deceived in the Garden of Eden. It is this target of the deception which I would like to highlight today—"the **simplicity** that is in Christ."

MY OWN RETURN TO GOD

When I returned to God, I remember opening up my Bible with a fresh new mindset of desiring to know what God has to say to me. I was eager to learn what changes God wanted me to make in my life. I had laid down my old life to God and yearned to be remade in His image.

With the twenty-twenty vision of hindsight, I can now see the numerous mistakes I made in my search for God's instruction in my life. There were many instances in which I read right over God's answer for a particular problem I was dealing with without even realizing it. The truth I was searching for was concealed within its simplicity.

I had problems evolving from covetousness, and I didn't recognize God's simple solution of "being thankful" (Ephesians 5:3, 4). I had marriage difficulties that persisted until I realized and accepted the simple instruction of Ephesians 5:25 to love my wife like Jesus loves the Church. I was frequently defeated by bitterness until I yielded to the simple truth contained in Hebrews 12:14, 15. In each of the situations above, I had overlooked God's simple expressed prescription, and that caused delay in receiving the healing I was seeking from Him.

SEARCHING FOR SIMPLICITY

Jesus's instructions for us are never complicated, and we should hone our expectations into looking for the simple solutions. We need to be on guard against being dismissive of the simple things contained within the Bible. It is essential to read the Bible with a deliberate thoughtfulness, coupled with an open heart to the Holy Spirit for guidance. When we submit our hearts and mind to God, He will reward us with the truth that we are looking for.

Although Jesus' instructions may be simple, they are rarely easy. Proverbs 3:5 (Day 1) instructs us to, "Trust in the Lord with all thine heart; and lean not unto thine own understanding." The instruction given is very simple to understand, but performing the task is difficult and requires discipline and commitment on our part. It is at this point that we must turn our faith into trust; we must walk out what we confess to believe.

How do we do that? We must be obedient to the calling of the Holy Spirit, and lay down any notion of interfering with God's plan. We need to accept the simple instructions given throughout the Bible, and ask God to help us accomplish them in our life. God does not expect us to change on our own accord and ability; He wants us to trust Him completely to make the changes in us that He desires.

Finally, I encourage you to strengthen your faith by walking out God's simple instructions. God is our all-knowing Father who has detailed the simple instructions for all His sons and daughters to have life more abundantly (John 10:10). The many truths contained within the Bible are established to help break the shackles that bind you. Freedom from addiction and sin are just a simple step of obedience away!

Day 15

Matthew 6:33 - But seek ye first the kingdom of God, and His righteousness; and all these things shall be added unto you.

THE BEGINNING OR our third week in this discipleship journey brings us to a very personal verse for me—Matthew 6:33. In this verse, Jesus issues the simple solution to a practical problem which plagues many people within the churches.

I grew up in a low-income household. My mother made many of my clothes and cut my hair. My shoes would literally be falling apart before I would get new ones, and we couldn't afford cafeteria lunches at school. Our family progressed into a lower middle class as I grew older, but, by then, I had ingrained into me an unhealthy aspiration to succeed financially. My desire to be wealthy shaped every decision that I made and every relationship I allowed to develop.

Even when I came back to God, I initially held back my professional life from His authority. I gave God dominion over my personal life, but I didn't submit my businesses to Him. I mistakenly assumed that I needed to provide for myself and my family. I was obedient in how I used the money I earned, but I didn't know how to trust God to provide for me.

THE 2008 FINANCIAL CRISIS

In 2008, the world watched as the biggest banks throughout the world started failing one after another. This financial crisis originated from the real estate market in the United States, in which all my businesses were rooted. All at once, my ability to earn a living stopped completely!

God had been speaking with me, letting me know that I was about to go through this storm, but I wouldn't listen. I attempted to negotiate with Him to no avail. I promised to do this or that if He would protect me from losing the businesses I leaned upon, but He continued to warn me of the forthcoming change in my future.

I remember being so worried about having to terminate all my employees, which included many family members and friends. I was engulfed with fear and stress, and my previous prayers were not being answered in the way I wanted them to be. I went down to my knees for another attempt to bargain with God, and He again let me know that I was going to go through this storm which I feared; but, this time, I heard Him say in my spirit, "I will be with you, so trust Me."

GOD'S GRACE IN MY LIFE

It was in that moment that I gave one hundred percent of my life to God, including my income decisions. For the first time in my life, I did not know how I would earn a living. With 700,000 net jobs a month being lost in the United States, the outlook for new employment was miserable. I didn't know what I was going to do, but now that I was trusting in God, I truly walked without fear and stress.

I was drawn to Matthew 6 and the explicit promise contained in verse 33. I was comforted with the affirmation that God understands that we need certain material things to provide for our families. I cherished the pledge in verse 33 that "all these things should be added unto you." This verse validated what the voice I had heard in my spirit say to me when I laid down my fear. It increased my faith that God would supply all my needs.

There is a preliminary condition which we must comply with before we can expect God's blessing—"But seek ye first the kingdom of God." We must put God first in honor and ranking within our lives. God needs to be our highest priority without wavering or compromise.

As I look back at the eight years since then, I can jubilantly convey to you that God has faithfully provided for me at every step of the way. He has been generous to me and my family more times than I can remember. God has taken my cold and empty life filled with deadlines, stress, and vanity, and He has replaced it with purpose, peace, and family.

Is your faith for your welfare in worldly things like wealth and success? Do you trust God to provide the necessities of life for you? I encourage you to give God one hundred percent dominion over your life and seek His kingdom first above all. Go to Him now with a repenting heart and put your full trust in Him for your needs.

Day 16

Psalms 32:10 - Many sorrows shall be to the wicked: but he that trusteth in the LORD, mercy shall compass him about.

THE VERSE ABOVE fills my heart with hope and joy every time I read it, because it promises mercy to those who trust in God. God's mercy is something that I value immensely.

I remember a conversation I had with my mother while I was studying *The Book of Psalms* back in 2010. I had conveyed to her that I didn't enjoy this book as much as I did the others because of the poetic structure of the composition. My mother smiled at me and wisely responded with, "Oh, son, you will someday!" She was absolutely correct.

I have since permanently incorporated reading a chapter of Psalms into my daily schedule because of the wonderful encouragement I receive from it. *The Book of Psalms* is overflowing with promises and assurances intended to inspire the sons and daughters of God. Today's verse is emblematic of the numerous occasions in Psalms where God's wonderful promises to those of us that love and trust Him are expressed.

MERCY

I do not want to complicate the message contained in this verse; it simply states that God's mercy will surround each person who trusts in Him. How many times in your life have you been in a position where you needed mercy? I make so many mistakes in my effort to live my life in accordance with God's instructions that it would be a futile endeavor without God's endless mercy available to me.

Whenever frustrations cause me to react angrily to my children, God's mercy is there to correct me. Whenever bitterness creeps into my marriage, God's mercy is there to restore me. Whenever fear of future's uncertainty is permitted to reign in my heart, God's mercy is there to renew me. No matter how many times we fail in our efforts to walk in God's righteousness, His mercies are there to establish and fill us.

FAITH IN ACTION

As with many of God's promises and blessings, there is a qualifier attached. In this particular verse, the qualifier is, "He that trusteth in the LORD." We earlier defined trust as putting our faith into action (Day 1). If we have faith in an instruction from God, that faith becomes trust when we act upon it. We must act upon the instructions of God in order to be surrounded with His mercy.

For you to be reading this book today, it would be likely that you have put your faith in our Lord and Savior, Jesus Christ. I ask you to make a passionate decision today to turn that faith into trust. Make a determined effort to walk the path that God lays out in front of you. Accept His truths expressed in the Bible, and do not be detoured by your own rationale. When you do this, you are promised that God's amazing and generous mercies will encompass you all around.

Day 17

> 2 Corinthians 10:5 - Casting down imaginations, and every high thing that exalteth itself against the knowledge of God, and bringing into captivity every thought to the obedience of Christ;

ARE YOU STRUGGLING with an addiction or a sin that seems to continuously creep back into your mind? If you answered "yes," then our verse today is for you.

In the movie *Fireproof*, Kirk Cameron stars as a firefighter that is losing his marriage over anger, selfishness, and an addiction to pornography. The movie catalogs how Kirk Cameron's character, Caleb Holt, addresses the works of his flesh as he adopts the godly instruction contained in a book his father gives him as encouragement to fight for his marriage.

There is this one scene in the movie that is particularly relevant to our verse today. Caleb is sitting at his home computer doing some work when an X-rated website ad pops up on his screen. You can see the internal battle raging within Caleb's mind as he instinctively starts to move his mouse toward the icon. There is a difficult pause as Caleb's intensifying lust collides with the recently read biblical counsel to rid himself of the sinful obstacles and temptations which have damaged his marriage. Finally, Caleb dashes outside with his computer hard drive and proceeds to pummel it with a baseball bat.

TAKING OUR THOUGHTS CAPTIVE

Caleb was, in fact, acting out 2 Corinthians 10:5 by taking captive the instrument through which the lure of pornography reached him. Our instruction is to "cast down" the sinful desires that wrestle in our hearts. For Caleb, along with many other men, that sinful stronghold was pornography. We need to identify things and people which act as enticements to sin against God and purge them out of our lives. Caleb purged the access to the internet out of his home.

Notice the instruction in the verse to fight the battle of sin at the first thought in our mind. If the thought is contrary to the obedience of Jesus Christ, then we are directed to seize it immediately. Our ability to conquer temptations is optimum at the very moment in which the thought of sin is recognized. Every second we allow the sinful thought to remain in our mind, we become more and more susceptible to its power. We become weakened as we consider the sinful appeals and soon find ourselves vulnerable as we rationalize what we know we should not do.

THE SERMON ON THE MOUNT

Jesus' Sermon on the Mount offers a greater understanding to our Day 17 verse when Jesus warns us that if we even look on someone with lust, we have committed adultery in our heart (Matthew 5:27-29). He goes on to say that if your eye is causing you to commit adultery by lusting after someone, then you should pluck it out and cast it away. Jesus is teaching us to attack sin at the initial point where the lust begins, which in this example was the eye.

Is there a sin that has a hold on you? Do you find yourself justifying reasons to keep that sin in your life? If you said "yes" to both of these questions, you are not alone. I ask that you take a cue from Caleb Holt and purge your surroundings from the enticements of sin that have taken a stronghold in your life. Seek God in prayer with an admission of what you are battling, and ask Him to give you power over it. Ask God to give you warning of anything that would lure you back to that sin.

Day 18

Romans 8:28 - And we know that all things work together for good to them that love God, to them who are the called according to his purpose.

TODAY'S VERSE IS an extremely important weapon in our spiritual battle, a weapon we must never leave home without. We will wield this verse whenever we are face-to-face with hardships and adversities, when we are struggling with the reasons why something terrible happened, or when we are straining to see the possibility of joy past the circumstances at hand.

Dr. Missler, of Koinonia House, was the first person I ever heard speak of his own personal affection for this verse. He shared the struggles he experienced as his multi-national companies went bankrupt. Many people suffered financial loss, and his reputation was soiled; he and his family were ostracized by everyone, including by members and friends at his home church. These events culminated in his serious consideration of suicide until a dear friend pointed him to Romans 8:28.

A PROFOUND PROMISE FROM GOD

This verse, like many others we have reviewed, contains a promise from God with a qualifier. Let's begin with the promise from God:

> "And we know that all things work together for good…"

The verse proclaims that all things <u>work</u> for good, not that all things <u>are</u> good. In Dr. Missler's case, bankruptcy was not good, but the promise from God was that his bankruptcy would <u>work</u> for good. He could trust that God was doing something good in his life with the bankruptcies.

In fact, because of the bankruptcy, Dr. Missler ended up founding an internet-based Bible school along with two physical campuses. He has written numerous commentaries on the Bible and is a highly-sought-after public speaker; he has affected the spiritual lives of tens of thousands of serious Bible students. Although he couldn't understand why he was going through those incredible difficulties at the time of his bankruptcy, God had a higher calling for him. God was transitioning Dr. Missler out of the business world and into the great ministries that he eventually established.

THE QUALIFIER

God's promise that all things will work for good does not apply to everyone. It only applies to:

> "…them that love God, to them who are the called according to his purpose."

Bad things happen to people all the time and nothing good will happen from those events, but for those people who love God, we can be confident that God will bring good from terrible things in life.

In 2008, the world's financial system crashed as a consequence of an unrestrained United States' real estate banking system. All of my successful businesses were rooted in that devastated real estate market, and I was compelled to shut everything down. I incurred great financial loss, terminated jobs of friends and family, and was stripped of my own ability to earn an income.

God had a better plan for me. He wanted me to assemble my extended family together to weather the effects of the great recession. He also gave me a significant amount of free time to study the Bible. God was preparing me to lead prison and jail ministries. Most importantly, God was strengthening me spiritually and teaching me how to depend exclusively upon Him. I have a thriving, loving, and deep relationship with God because of the personal storm that I went through.

Are you going through something incredibly difficult? Are you struggling to see the light at the end of the tunnel? I want you to receive the divine comfort and full assurance from God that is available to all who love God. He has promised you to make good out of whatever tribulation you are currently going through.

I urge you to open your heart to God by divulging your fears and concerns to Him. Ask God to show you the good that He has in store for your life. Ask Him for the faith and guidance to walk the path that He has in store for you. Then trust God to do the good which He promised to do for you.

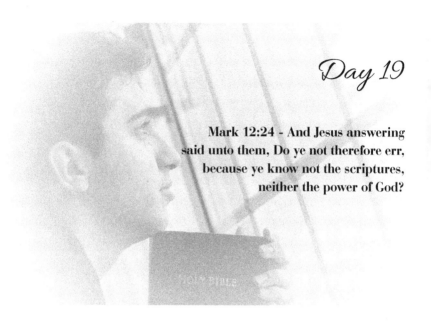

Day 19

Mark 12:24 - And Jesus answering said unto them, Do ye not therefore err, because ye know not the scriptures, neither the power of God?

IN THE MANY opportunities I've had to minister to men in prison, jail, rehabilitation facilities, and churches, I have found the truth contained in Mark 12:24 to be fundamental and necessary to the long-term success in a person's walk with God. Let me start by suggesting something that may sound controversial—an individual can be "saved" and still go through their entire life in the bondage of sin and addiction.

We receive forgiveness of our sins when we believe in our heart that God raised Jesus from the dead and we confess Jesus as our Lord and Savior with our mouth (Romans 10:9, 10). If a person does not yield to the conviction of the Holy Spirit, or the Word of God, that person will return to the sin and addiction that constrained them before (Proverbs 26:11). If, however, a person yields their own self will to God's will, then that person will spend a lifetime being molded into the image of Jesus Christ (2 Corinthians 3:18; Romans 8:29; Colossians 3:10).

THE ERROR

Jesus diagnoses the cause of the hard hearts of the religious leaders in this verse by proclaiming their error. Jesus tells them that their reasoning is flawed because they do not know the scriptures (Bible). Even though these religious leaders had spent a lifetime in the pursuit of leading religious activities, they did not *know* the Bible. They knew the religious rules, the stories, and the commentaries of religious leaders, but they didn't know the heart and purpose of God.

Jesus links a consequence to those who do not know the scriptures—they will not know the power of God. Here is revealed the arduous obstacle for many religious people in realizing the healing power of God. Many people do not read the Bible with a desire to hear God speak unto them. Throughout the Bible we are counseled to read His Word every day (Matthew 6:11; Acts 2:46; Acts 17:11), not just once a week on Sundays. His Word is spiritual food which we must consume daily in order not to starve.

Those who do not read their Bible daily are in jeopardy of not hearing or observing the Holy Spirit's convictions. They do not hear God speaking into their daily activities. As a result, they do not experience God's miraculous power to heal addictions, restore relationships, achieve victory in the battles of work and life, and receive the amazing peace that only comes from God.

MY OWN SELF ANALYSIS

When I became serious in my walk with God, I altered my daily routine with a purpose of installing good spiritual habits. I introduced into my daily schedule morning and evening appointments for Bible reading and prayer time. There were occasions when I succumbed to the trials of work and life, allowing them to crowd out my time with God. As a result, I experienced angry reactions to frustrations along with a palpable absence of joy and peace. In my effort to explore the source of these negative qualities re-appearing in me, I realized that I had been derelict in keeping my new schedule for some time, and I immediately went to prayer for relief.

In my opportunities of ministering to countless men in prison, I have heard a very familiar story repeated often by so many. I would hear reports about how well they were once doing along with details of going to church, praying, and reading the Bible. When asked about what changed for them, they would all tell me they stopped reading their Bible for some reason or another. We can see very clearly that they "erred" from the power of God in the manner which Jesus had warned the religious leaders in our verse above.

Let's take Jesus' warning very seriously by guarding the daily appointments we have with Him in reading the Bible and praying. Be protective in not allowing the concerns of life, nor the lures of the world to supplant our priority time with God. Pledge now to start each morning with a prayer and a Bible reading. Let's seek God before we do anything else each day, thereby assuring that we will experience the "power of God!"

Day 20

Psalms 86:5 - For thou, Lord, art good, and ready to forgive; and plenteous in mercy unto all them that call upon thee.

WE DISCUSSED GOD'S attribute of never ending mercy back on Day 3 with Lamentations 3:23, but I feel strongly that we must defend this truth from the relentless attacks of Satan to convince us otherwise.

The word mercy appears 276 times in 261 verses in the King James Version, and the vast majority of them are describing the magnitude of God's love for us. You can hardly find a book of the Bible in which God's attribute of mercy is not explicitly expressed. The following statement about God's mercy is repeated eleven separate times in nearly identical form (1 Chr. 16:34, 41; Ezra 3:11; Ps. 106:1; 107:1; 118:1, 29; 136:1-3; 136:26):

> O give thanks unto the LORD; for he is good;
> for his mercy endureth for ever.

SATAN'S MOTIVE

Satan will do anything he can to hinder our walk with God. One tactic that I've experienced personally is that he endeavors to discourage me with my failures by attempting to deceitfully convince me that God is mad at me. He wants me to feel isolated and alone, thinking that God has abandoned me. Embarrassment, shame, and frustration are the weapons he uses.

I've also seen the successful effect which Satan has had in numerous other people. I've been face-to-face with men when they have exhaustively voiced their resignation in defeat. In their struggles, they believe Satan's lie over God's truth. They believed that they blew their opportunity and were unworthy of God. They rationalized that since God was finished with them, they might as well quit trying.

MY BEST FRIEND'S PERSONAL EXPERIENCE

I met my best friend, Jason, attending my Bible study at Omega Technical Violator Center (a low security correctional facility). He was serving his fourth prison sentence for a felony probation violation when he heard the Holy Spirit speak to him during a study on *The Book of Revelation*. Inspired by God, Jason made a decision to submit completely to God and yield to His will.

Upon his release from prison, Jason's life consisted of a bedroom at his grandmother's home, mounting court fines, no job, a huge car payment he couldn't afford, and a girl-friend who had just had his baby. In the face of those overwhelming pressures, Jason sought God to provide for all his needs. One of Jason's first acts of obedience to God was to marry his girlfriend Keri.

Jason received sporadic work here and there, enough to provide for immediate needs. Soon afterwards, God blessed Jason with an opportunity to own his own business as a siding installer for a major local company. A while later, God blessed Jason with his own home large enough to accommodate his new bride, their daughter, and their new son growing inside of Keri. Jason's love for God was openly evident to anyone who knew him, especially the men at a local rehabilitation facility where Jason spoke once a week.

Then something unfortunate happened—Jason went to jail because of a DWI. I remember the deafening silence of Jason's text refusing to talk to me about what was happening. His shame and embarrassment pushed him into isolation. He would later tell me that he had considered quitting his walk with God, to just go back to his old life. He thought God was mad at him.

Fortunately, Jason would soon defeat Satan's attack by going to God in focused prayer seeking His mercy. I noticed an immediate change in Jason as fear was replaced with God's peace. God was faithful to His promises and showered mercy upon Jason. This all cumulated in a court appearance for the DWI. For a normal person, a DWI is a serious ordeal, but for a four-time felon, a DWI could result in a long prison sentence.

I accompanied Jason to court and stood next to him as a character witness. What I saw next can only be described as God's divine love direct from heaven. By a series of strange circumstances, a different judge was serving that day; a judge who knew Jason personally and was very familiar with the great changes in Jason's life. God placed this judge there that day to be His vessel to pour His mercy on Jason by allowing Jason to work during the daytime, and serve his minimum jail sentence at night.

Over the following months, God's mercies continued to accumulate in Jason's life. He just recently received his third child (second son), and he has matured greatly as a brother in Christ. There have been numerous people inspired by Jason's personal testimony who have been led to seek Jesus's love for themselves.

Do you have a need for God's mercy in your life? God wants you to know that He is full of mercy for you, and He is generous in giving of it. He is ready to forgive all those that seek it, and His reservoir of mercy for you is overflowing.

Day 21

> **Proverbs 9:10 - The fear of the LORD is the beginning of wisdom: and the knowledge of the holy is understanding.**

IN THE DAY 2 chapter, we read the famous quote from Chinese philosopher Lao Tzu, "The journey of a thousand miles begins with a single step." I want to acknowledge and congratulate you on reaching the half-way mark of your forty-day spiritual growth journey with this book.

I recall, as a young boy, being quite envious of Solomon's distinguished moment when he asked God for wisdom instead of riches, wealth, or honor (2 Chronicles 1:10, 11). Solomon had asked for wisdom to perform God's will in judging and ruling over God's people, rather than something that would enrich himself. God was pleased with Solomon and rewarded him with riches, wealth, and honor in addition to unequaled wisdom.

AN OVERDUE PRAYER

Later, as I began my new walk with God, I voiced to friends my desire to please God in a manner similar to Solomon, requesting wisdom instead of riches. My whole life had previously been a pursuit of riches, and I regretted that I had not lived worthy of God. Each time I expressed this sentiment, I became more and more troubled in my spirit. My agitation finally fled when I realized the obvious—I can *STILL* pray for wisdom now!

That specific petition occupied my prayers for many days. I found comfort in James 1:5 which promises abundant wisdom to everyone who asks God for it. I soon noticed joy emerging where regret once dwelled. Consequently, I became immersed in Bible studies. For the first time, I was able to understand the character and heart of God through the events recorded in the Bible.

WISDOM'S FRUIT

Over time, I began growing deep in my relationship with God, and I matured spiritually. This was all a product of God rewarding me with an answered prayer for wisdom. The more wisdom I received, the greater God became to me. That observation was realized one day when the Holy Spirit put today's verse in front of me, "The fear of the LORD is the beginning of wisdom." I recognized the link between the presence of "the fear of the Lord" in my own life and the increasing awareness I was having of how great God is. I was growing in "the fear of the Lord" because God was giving me wisdom.

I mark my prayer for wisdom and the subsequent gift by God as a defining moment in my spiritual growth. God had instilled in me a great desire to know His Word and His heart. The closer I get to God, the more I realize how far away from Him we really are. I do not want to ever be satisfied with the current status of my relationship with God as it stands at any point. I want to continue to grow closer to Him and to know Him deeper.

I have also discovered that the majority of my views and perceptions have changed dramatically since then. I have found incredible value in spiritual things where many others will abandon for convenience and comfort. Conversely, I have also come to know that many traditions and institutions I once valued were, in fact, in opposition to me and my God.

Are you in need of more of God's wisdom? Are you concerned about the longevity of your walk with God? Take today's verse to heart and realize that we need to have an exalted respect for God and who He is. When we "fear the Lord," we are dropping all restraints on His Holy Spirit to work in our lives. When we "fear the Lord," we open ourselves to be completely molded to His will. Ask God now for a liberal helping of His incredible wisdom!

Day 22

Psalms 37:3-5 - Trust in the LORD, and do good; so shalt thou dwell in the land, and verily thou shalt be fed.

Delight thyself also in the LORD; and He shall give thee the desires of thine heart.

Commit thy way unto the LORD; trust also in Him; and He shall bring it to pass.

I WANT TO begin our fourth week with one of my favorite selections of verses describing God's instruction to us on how to have our needs realized by Him.

I first heard of the fabricated acronym for the BIBLE, **B**asic **I**nstruction **B**efore **L**eaving **E**arth, from an inmate at one of my Bible studies. I was instantly charmed by it because of its accurateness. The Bible is an instruction manual given to us by our Father in heaven, a Father who has been separated from His children because of their sin. The Bible is our Father's love letter to us, designed to guide His lost children back home to Him.

PERCEPTION CORRECTION

When I was growing up in church during the late seventies and the early eighties, I had an incorrect perception of God. I pictured

God sitting on His throne in heaven watching everyone on Earth just waiting for me to mess up. I was inundated with preaching that presented God as requiring absolute perfection from me, and I was increasingly aware of how imperfect I was. Each time I acknowledged my sin, I would separate myself further from God.

Later in life, an attentive reading of the Bible corrected my misunderstanding very rapidly. I soon observed a constant theme throughout the Bible depicting God's heart to love and forgive us. He is constantly demonstrating mercy, grace, and forgiveness to all who sincerely ask for it. The Bible is overflowing with instruction on how to be blessed by God and how to receive God's provision for our needs.

Our verses today list three separate significant promises from God along with simple instructions on how to obtain them. Like most of the occurrences within the Bible, God's blessings are accompanied with a condition. You do this, and God will do that. It requires an act of faith from us to receive God's promised blessing.

GOD'S PETITION TO US TO TRUST HIM

The promises contained in these three verses are reaching into the faith of the believer to trust God for the long-term. They are promises which signify assurance to us that God will not abandon us. They promise that trust now will be rewarded for the duration. Let's take a closer look:

PROMISE

1) God will provide daily provision and shelter.
2) God will fulfill the godly desires of your heart.
3) God repeats His resilient assurance of doing what He says.

CONDITION

1) Trust God, and do what is good.
2) Enjoy your relationship with God.
3) Make a pledge to follow and trust God.

I do not want to go through life depending on my own ability to provide food, shelter, clothing, and medical treatment for my family. I want to know that God will always be there to deliver the necessities of life for my family, so I am greatly comforted by Psalm 37:3-5. Are you?

Verse 4 promises the desires of your heart. I have a desire in my heart to have an active life with my wife and children. I want to be an integral part of their lives and the lives of their future husbands and children. I want to see generations of Kimbles worshipping God together, and Psalm 37:4 feeds my hope. What is the desire of your heart?

Day 23

James 4:8 - Draw nigh to God, and He will draw nigh to you. Cleanse your hands, ye sinners; and purify your hearts, ye double minded.

I JUST FINISHED viewing *God's Not Dead 2*, and I was inspired to include this next verse by one of the moments in the movie. The main character, Grace Wesley, is going through a very difficult legal trial because she answered a question about Jesus when asked by one of her students in the classroom. In the midst of her legal adversity, Grace nervously expresses to her grandfather that she cannot feel God's presence. She felt isolated; she felt alone.

I was thankful for that line in the movie because I believe that it is something we all experience at times in our lives. I have had several instances when I felt the same way as Grace. I would be seeking God's help with a difficult circumstance, and it just seemed like God was nowhere to be found.

A SPIRITUAL INSTRUCTION

James 4:8 is very simple and straight to the point, which is a trait that I appreciate. "Draw near to God, and He will draw near to you." This simple instruction has been proven over and over again in my own prayer life. I have wrestled with routine as it attempts to mutate sincerity in my prayer and Bible reading times with monotonous repetition. In this struggle, I am victorious when I apply this verse.

I step back in my prayer and concentrate on God. I look at all the situations and worries in my life with the realization that they are putting distance between God and me. I put these concerns aside and deliberately concentrate on Him alone. I verbally acknowledge His love for me as He offered His Son on the Cross for my sins. I target my thoughts to God's love for me with a purpose of drawing near to Him, and God has faithfully responded every time by drawing near to me!

GRACE WESLEY'S ISOLATION

Back to the movie and the fictional situation of Grace Wesley; she was feeling isolated from God at a time when she was being persecuted for defending Jesus. This understandably brought concern and anxiety in her life as she pondered the question of "why?" Why was she going through this, and why did God allow all this hate to be directed towards her?

The movie didn't answer these questions directly, but we see God's plan revealed in the end. God had a greater purpose to reach many of the students, lawyers, teachers, and jurors through Grace's faith. The way Grace stayed true to her faith when so many people were attacking her refusal to compromise culminated with a dramatic demonstration of God's love and power over the world's hate and weakness. Grace needed to stop and look at her circumstances through God's eyes.

James 4:8 is the instruction for anyone who is going through something similar to Grace's situation. We should approach God in prayer and put the burden at His feet. We should draw near to God and voice our trust in His providence over our lives. We should ask Him to reveal His plan for us and seek His strength and power to endure whatever hardship we are experiencing.

I encourage you to memorize James 4:8 and hide it in your heart (Psalms 119:11). Whenever you feel far away from God, realize that He didn't leave you—you drifted away from God. Take out this verse from your memory and put it into action. Quote it to God in prayer, and draw near to Him. He promises to draw near to you!

Day 24

Song of Songs 4:7 (NKJV) - You are all fair, my love, And there is no spot in you.

THIS VERSE IS a favorite of my pastor's wife, Tanner, who incorporates it into so many publications and marketing materials for women's events at our church. I became fond of this verse after seeing one of Tanner's brochures pinned on my refrigerator day after day.

The verse affirms the reader's value and image in God's eyes by declaring that we are all beautifully and wonderfully created (Psalms 139:14). Unfortunately, the vast majority of women do not see themselves in a similar way. I recall a sermon in which my pastor spoke about what women see when they look in a mirror. Instead of seeing their beauty, they see flaws. There is a whole industry of retail companies, magazine publishers, and beauty product manufacturers that are prospering on the insecurities of women.

THE VERSE GETS PERSONAL

Soon afterwards, I was watching TV in the bedroom while my wife was getting ready in front of the full length mirror. I was astonished as I heard her voice flaw after flaw which she perceived to see in the reflection. All of a sudden, that sermon became very real to me. A beautiful woman, whose appearance I have always communicated my delight in, saw only faults and blemishes.

I realized that I needed to speak God's truth into my wife and my two young daughters, one of which is dealing with a significant learning disability. I've seen this daughter, Sydney, hurt by the derisive taunting of kids pouncing on the deviation of what everyone perceives to be normal. The criticisms she endures could have a long-lasting negative effect, but God gave me this verse as a tool for me to take action. I was determined to have my girls hear their father speak the same words that our heavenly Father speaks to us all, "You are altogether beautiful."

GOD VALIDATES THIS TRUTH TO ME

Shortly after this revelation, I took a trip with a mentor and friend of mine, Chaplain Bradford (Chap). He was the chaplain of the prison in which I volunteered, and he was instrumental in God's molding of me as a ministry leader. We were taking a thirteen-hour car ride to South Carolina for a convention, and we had many deep conversations about God and shared personal testimonies (Revelation 12:11). One story Chap shared was used by God to speak directly to me!

Chap revealed that in his previous marriage, he and his wife had a daughter named Melody. Melody was born with such a severe handicap, that she could not even roll over in bed on her own ability. Melody's impairment came with enormous needs that had life-changing effects on her parents. Unfortunately, Melody's mother became bitter and self-absorbed, and she sought an escape.

Chap's heart was hurting for Melody in many ways. He was hurting from the handicap that his daughter was living with, and he was hurting from the lack of affection from her mother. The pain was overwhelming to Chap as he bore the anguish of his daughter, and he asked God why He didn't make his daughter normal. Chap said that God immediately responded clearly—"She **IS** normal for Melody."

Wow! I was moved by that story, and it confirmed the truth from our verse. Melody was altogether beautiful in God's eyes, and God comforted Chap into seeing that as well. Through Chap's testimony, I was greatly heartened to appreciate God's truth in Sydney as well. I am no longer sympathetic for Sydney because of her disability; Sydney is exactly how God created her. God created her with a heart bigger than the state of Texas, and I want her to know that she is altogether beautiful every day of her life.

God wants you to know that you are not a mistake. You were created in His image, and He finds you beautiful and flawlessly made!

Day 25

Hebrews 13:5, 6 (NKJV) - Let your conduct be without covetousness; be content with such things as you have. For He Himself has said, "I will never leave you nor forsake you."

So we may boldly say: "The LORD is my helper; I will not fear. What can man do to me?"

TODAY'S VERSE BEST encapsulates the key components from a detailed study of a topic the Bible has much to say about—*FEAR*. There are at least 366 variations within the Bible instructing the reader not to fear.

Our culture does not permit men to acknowledge their fear. Fear is categorized as a weakness which society asks men to eliminate with courage and bravery. We celebrate the attributes of valor and boldness in man and link those attributes to success. This results in the celebration of man while eliminating the glory of God. We subtly replace God with courage; we glorify the creature instead of the Creator (Romans 1:25).

FAITH INSTEAD OF BRAVERY

In Mark 4:40, Jesus diagnosed the disciples fear from a lack of faith. Faith is the opposite of fear: faith in the Word of God. Men and women do great things when they act in faith on what God moves them to do. From the outside looking in, these acts of faith appear to others as bravery or courage. Our verse above supports this conclusion when it says, "So we may boldly say: 'The Lord is my helper; I will not fear.'" We can be bold because we have faith that God will do what He says He will do.

The Bible teaches us that we overcome fear by trusting in God. The Word of God is filled with promises to provide His people with protection, provision, and to meet their needs. When we believe what God says in His Word, we call this faith. When we walk out our faith in the world, fear is defeated, allowing the man or woman of God to successfully perform His will. The faithful man or woman then glorifies God, not pilfering the credit or accolades for themselves.

PROMISES FROM GOD

Satan's primary tactic to defeat us is to get us to doubt God's Word (Genesis 3:1 / Day 10). A closed Bible for any duration is an indication that Satan is succeeding. When we allow ourselves to be distracted from reading the Bible, we make ourselves more susceptible to believing his lies. Lies such as:

- God is mad at you.
- God is too busy for you.
- God doesn't know you.
- You have to fend for yourself because God doesn't care about you.

Those lies generate great fear in us, and that fear drives us to bondage. We can defeat those attacks on us by recalling and believing God's promise to never abandon us. Verse 5 above is standing upon a previous promise of God to "never leave you nor forsake you" in Deuteronomy 31:6, 8. This specific promise of God is repeated several times, including the following -

> "...I will fear no evil: for thou art with me..." - **Psalm 23:4**

> "...whom shall I fear? the LORD is the strength of my life..." - **Psalm 27:1**

> "...and the LORD is with us: fear them not." - **Numbers 14:9**

Are you exhausted from coping alone with the fears in your life? Does it seem like when one fear is vanquished, two other fears arrive in its place? God did not put that fear in your life; in fact, He wants to take it from you! Seize this moment right now to acknowledge your fears to God. Ask God to speak His truth to you about any specific fear that you are dealing with. He promises to overcome it. Will you trust Him?

Day 26

Matthew 6:21 - For where your treasure is, there will your heart be also.

IF YOU HAVE spent any amount of time in church, you have probably heard of today's verse. It is one of those verses chosen to be put onto bookmarks, greeting cards, and many other Christian novelty gifts. It is a verse that most church people will acknowledge knowing; however, most of them (like I once did) have it backwards.

Simplicity is a great cloak for profound truth to hide under, and this verse illustrates that concept perfectly. This verse is so small and simple that most readers assume they already understand the message being conveyed, without stopping to ponder the implications. Let's be cautious to avoid falling into a similar trap and read the verse again slowly:

"For where your treasure is, there will your heart be also."

CAUSE AND EFFECT

What Jesus is revealing here is that the thing we treasure directs our hearts. Our heart is guided by what we treasure, rather than our treasure being guided by our heart. This detail is significant in order for us to make the necessary changes in our life. Jesus is delineating the cause and effect relationship preventing many people from inheriting His blessing of peace and joy.

Why is this important? Have you ever been "in love" with someone who you knew wasn't good for you? If so, then you realize how difficult it is to go against what your heart yearns for. We have all experienced defeat in trying to be disciplined against our heart when our mind's reason told us otherwise. A quote by the famous American poet Emily Dickinson demonstrates surrender in defeat of the heart with, "The heart wants what it wants—or else it does not care."

CHANGE FROM TRUTH

Like so many others, I treasured money. Although I loved God, and I did receive His gift of salvation, I treasured money's ability to provide for me and my family. I prayed to God for His blessing upon my businesses, and I tithed in obedience to His instructions, but I treasured money's benifits over God. I didn't realize it at the time, but I was serving money and its obligations.

I was convicted upon reading this verse, but I didn't understand the truth Jesus was conveying to me. The Holy Spirit was saying, "Rob, turn your treasure from money unto Jesus, and your heart will follow." Regrettably, I needed God to do something drastic before I would listen. I needed Him to take everything away from me so that the only option I had was to trust in Him.

As I relied on God for everything in my life, I rapidly became enamored with His Word. Use of my limited funds shifted from items of vanity to purchasing Bible commentaries and books.

Next, I enrolled in a Bible school with an aggressive curriculum, which felt more like fun than work. I was treasuring God's Word, and my heart had followed!

What really surprised me were how many other things I had treasured above God. The Dallas Cowboys, Florida Gators, NASCAR, and my wife and kids were all things or people which I treasured above God. I still enjoy sports, but they are limited to simple entertainment for me now. They do not run my schedule or my emotional state. More importantly, I now see my wife and kids through God's eyes rather than my own. I understand His will for my family is much different and nobler than what was my will.

Do you have some unhealthy desires in your life? Are you in need of changing where your heart is? God is waiting for you to give Him your whole heart, and He will show you if you are in need of changing what you treasure. Ask Him to substitute any worldly desires with His Word. Ask Him to give you a passionate desire for His Word and His will.

Day 27

Ephesians 5:25 - Husbands, love your wives, even as Christ also loved the church, and gave Himself for it;

I HAVE GREAT affection for this verse because God used it to rescue my marriage from bitterness. This verse, specifically tailored for men, establishes a high standard for how husbands should love their wives. It is a standard that I am not able to accomplish on my own accord; a standard which I continually fall short of, but a standard which I have committed to strive for.

It was early within my second marriage, and I was accumulating bitterness to perceived shortcomings in my wife. I experienced unmet expectations from my wife as moments of betrayal within my mind. As a result, arguments multiplied and my criticisms became more hurtful. Consequently, we were living two separate lives in the same house with persistent negativity as the house guest that would not leave.

THE HOLY SPIRIT SPEAKS

My wife and I went to a church leadership group headed by our young new pastor, and we were masking the pain and isolation we were going through in our marriage. At one of these meetings, we were separated into groups by gender so we could discuss our roles as men and women. In my group, our pastor focused on conveying the Bible's instruction for husbands to lead their wives. This simple instruction felt like a conviction to which I frustratingly responded by asking, "How are we supposed to lead someone who doesn't want to be led?" I was convicted for giving up on leading my wife.

I went back home and read Ephesians 5 in search of God to speak to me about my marriage. When I read verse 25, the Holy Spirit revealed something profound to me. The verse instructs the husband to love his wife like Jesus loves His church. Jesus died for His church even though they were sinful and didn't deserve it. Men are put in both of the positions with this analogy. On the one hand, we are the husband to the wife, but on the other hand, we are the bride to Christ. If Jesus' love for me was conditional, subject to the same standard I was putting on my wife, then He would have given up on me a long time ago.

CHANGE OCCURS

I realized how provisional my love for my wife really was. I was so deficient from how God wanted me to love her. My spirit was renewed with a determination to rebuild our family. Whenever a situation occurred in which I felt she wasn't doing something *I wanted,* or not doing it as good as *I wanted,* I decided to sacrificially do it myself. I removed the situations that angered me by transforming them into opportunities to love my wife like Christ loved the church.

When any arguments returned, I realized the lasting pain

of the previous sharp criticisms I had heaped upon her. I took these occasions to acknowledge my hurtful words and to ask for forgiveness. God's work in me was continuous as He would address flaw after flaw in me. He was transforming me into a godly husband that He wanted for His daughter—Danielle Kimble.

Several months down the road I recognized something awesome. My wife was falling more in love with the man that I had become. Her respect for me was visibly apparent to the casual observer, and the arguments became scarce. The struggles I once had leading my wife in God's will evaporated once I allowed God to perform His will in me first.

Is your love for your spouse conditional? Is your marriage or relationship in need of a miracle from God? In this world we are always expecting satisfaction for our needs instead of searching for God's will for us. Make a decision today to remedy that. Ask God for His will in your relationship. Ask God to speak to you about the relationship that you are in or the relationship that He wants you in.

Day 28

> Romans 8:15 – For ye have not received the spirit of bondage again to fear; but ye have received the Spirit of adoption, whereby we cry, Abba, Father.

WE WILL FINISH our fourth week with an inspiring verse meant to encourage us to know our status and the relationship we have with God. I will not be able to fully caption the magnitude of the implications from this verse within the confinements of this book, but I hope to convey why I cherish the truths expressed. Let's start by breaking down three significant things we learn:

1) God doesn't give us the bondage (sin) which is what produces fear in our lives.
2) Our relationship with God is as a son or daughter. This is our new identity.
3) As a son or daughter, we approach God intimately as to a loving, concerned Father.

The first truth is that all of us have had something that shackled us. This bondage is a result of sin in our lives, and that bondage spawns fear in us. To many, this bondage manifests itself as an addiction to drugs, alcohol, or some other substance. To others, this bondage may appear in the form of bitterness or materialism. Whatever form the bondage assumes, it strengthens its grasp on the person through fear.

WE ARE ADOPTED

The verse informs the reader that we were delivered from our bondage when we were adopted as children of God. What a comfort to believers when we realize that the Living God looks upon us as His own children! His relationship with us is directed by an unshakable love for His kids. He genuinely and deeply wants you and I to experience the best life possible (John 10:10).

ADOPTION

Before I married my first wife, she was called about an opportunity to adopt her brother's wife's sister's new baby. I had rejected the initial idea until they put Sydney in my arms, at which point, I never let her go. I took her home with me across state lines and immediately arranged for the necessary legal adoption procedures. God has used this wonderful and beautiful daughter to draw me closer to Him. He has revealed absolute love, joy, kindness, through this special girl.

I have since experienced divorce and remarriage. Through this second marriage, God has generously blessed me with a second child through natural means. This daughter is equally special to me, and she has a unique zeal for life. She is filled with so much joy and innocence that unkindness is a foreign concept to her. While McKenzie is literally a part of me, there is not a difference in the love I have for my two daughters. I love them equally—blood and adopted alike.

OUR DAD

You and I are brothers and sisters in that we have been adopted by the same Father. When we accepted the gift of salvation through the blood of Jesus Christ, we were adopted into the family of the Creator of the universe. Our Father has great power, and his understanding is infinite (Psalms 147:5). His love for you and I is unconditional and unequaled. He is the perfect Dad!

God wants us to approach Him with that identity and intimacy. He wants us to recognize that the fear we experience comes from sin and that we should call upon Daddy (Abba) to overcome it. We have His incredible power and wisdom available to us at all times. We have a Father who is faithful, loving, merciful, mighty, generous, patient, and forgiving.

Are you still being harassed by fear from the bondage of your past? Reread this verse focusing on the truths of God being conveyed to you personally. Reach out to the open arms of your loving adoptive Daddy, and tell Him what has a grip on you. Trust Him to show you how to cast off the chains that bind you.

Day 29

James 3:14-16 - But if ye have bitter envying and strife in your hearts, glory not, and lie not against the truth.

This wisdom descendeth not from above, but is earthly, sensual, devilish.

For where envying and strife is, there is confusion and every evil work.

AS WE BEGIN our fifth week together, we will explore what the Bible has to say about something that touches each of us at varying times in our lives—*bitterness*. We are all susceptible to a severe and tangible risk from the influence of bitterness whether you are new believer, an unbeliever, or even an established pastor.

James informs us that bitterness reveals itself in the form of envying and conflict ("strife"). This information is essential in our effort to obtain an early diagnosis. If you experience envy of another person, or you are absorbed in a dispute with someone, you are exposed to bitterness and are in jeopardy of its potent venom.

THE SOURCE

Have you ever had a verbal quarrel with someone where you were left outraged? You replay the dispute over and over in your mind amplifying the insults and abuse you suffered. Soon, you embrace the anger and find consolation in thoughts of retaliation. You have an internal thought warning you of the destructive path you are about to travel, but that is quickly rejected in lieu of animosity. This is the "lie" which James tells us not to glory in. We are to listen to the still small voice warning us of impending hazard of bitterness.

Verse 15 informs us that "this wisdom" (reveling in our resentment and fanning the flames of our anger) does not come from God, but in fact, it is a tool of Satan. We can no longer feel righteous in our bitterness for others with the knowledge that the bitterness never comes from God. Hebrews 12:15 teaches us the bitterness grows like weeds and harms the individual who has it. Ephesians 4:31 instructs believers to dispose of all bitterness, wrath, anger, and evil speaking regardless of any justification for feeling that way. Colossians 3:19 commands husbands to not be bitter to their wives. These are all examples of the truth we should follow in verse 14.

A BARRIER TO HEALING

Early in my marriage, I held firm to bitterness towards my wife for occasions where I felt warranted. This bitterness multiplied at an incredible rate, and soon my wife could not make a simple mistake without me seizing upon it. The impact of my bitter feelings had a cancerous effect on me, my wife, and the marriage. My bitterness became a barrier to healing my marriage which was nearing a terminal stage.

When I took specific action in accordance with Colossians 3:19, God healed my marriage. When I followed Ephesians 4:31, I experienced His peace and resolution. When I observed Hebrews 12:15, I was able to defeat Satan's intended desires of harm on my marriage and relationships. Each of these victories was accomplished by yielding to God's truth and warnings about bitterness.

In my ministry, I repeatedly encounter bitter people who cannot see the love of Jesus through their scars from harmful actions of family members or friends. The more I speak of the forgiveness of Jesus, the more they speak of their pain. They are unable to consider the healing power of Jesus available to them, as they are solely consumed with blaming others and seeking pity.

Are you experiencing bitterness and discord for people in your life? Have you realized the damaging effects of responding to bitterness' cruel and callous purpose? Do you want God to heal your pain and relationships? God's instruction on bitterness is simple and direct—drop it. Let go of your bitterness in full recognition of the truth revealed which is that bitterness is evil and harmful. It comes from Satan with an intention to destroy you. Choose to forgive others just as Christ chose to forgive you at great cost!

Day 30

> Revelation 3:7, 8 - And to the angel of the church in Philadelphia write; These things saith He that is holy, He that is true, He that hath the key of David, He that openeth, and no man shutteth; and shutteth, and no man openeth;
>
> I know thy works: behold, I have set before thee an open door, and no man can shut it: for thou hast a little strength, and hast kept my word, and hast not denied my name.

TODAY'S VERSES WILL take a little more effort from us in unpacking the weighty truths contained within them, but the outcome will warrant our endeavor with incredible inspiration and direction.

In verse 7, Jesus is speaking to the Church of Philadelphia. He identifies Himself as, "He that is holy, He that is true, He that hath the key of David, He that openeth, and no man shutteth; and shutteth, and no man openeth;" Jesus pulled this title of Himself directly from Isaiah 22:22 which describes Eliakim, who was given the keys to the throne room of the king. The "key of David" represents the ability of Eliakim to grant people access to the king.

THE APPLICATION

Can you imagine the power of being able to grant someone an audience with the President of the United States at your sole discretion? There is a reason that politicians spend millions of dollars, and in the case of President, a billion plus dollars to get the job. Politics is contaminated with the corruption of selling access and influence to those whom hold power.

Jesus is telling us that He is the one with the "key of David." He alone gives us access to the King—God the Father! Verse 8 tells us that Jesus, "Set before thee an open door, and no man can shut it." No matter where you are, you have an open door to a mighty God who loves you. You have immediate and unfiltered access to the Most High God whose power is unmatched and whose understanding is infinite (Psalm 147:5).

EXERCISING OUR POWER

One of the greatest disappointments I have when I look back on my own life is the complete abandonment of this incredible power which was available to me the whole time. I recall countless relationship failures I experienced because I didn't seek God's involvement. I can now observe the accumulation of years in which I suffered through the stress and consequences of financial struggles because I withheld all decisions from God's supervision. More importantly, I never realized the faithfulness, love, and power of God working in my life.

To this day, I am greatly encouraged by the realization that I can drop to my knees and enter the throne room of God Almighty at any hour of any day. The door to the King is always open to me. He is always available to hear my petitions and to direct my path in life. He is eagerly available to lead me to victories in the face of chaos and defeat, and with every triumph from heaven experienced, comes an increased faith and an amplified awe of God.

Have you been remiss in seeking God's governance over all areas of your life? You were given power as a child of God (John 1:12); and you must exercise that power in order to yield the inherent results. Receive this revelation with all seriousness, and make the substantive decision to bring all choices and desires to the King of Kings. Jesus died to give you this amazing access and status as a child of God. Don't squander that gift by doing life on your own. Seek God's will and lordship in prayer on a daily basis, and bring into fruition the promised victories of God.

Day 31

Romans 5:8, 9 - But God commendeth His love toward us, in that, while we were yet sinners, Christ died for us.

Much more then, being now justified by His blood, we shall be saved from wrath through Him.

OUR VERSE TODAY has always been one that I hold in my memory because it describes the immense love of God for you and me. Now, though, the verse is even more endearing to me because I received a revelation this year, and I would love to share it with you here.

I was reviewing for an upcoming Bible study I was teaching about the prophetic fulfillment of Jesus in every detail of the Passover Feast. I had taught this particular lesson several times in both the local county jail and the state prison facility. It is always exciting for me to observe people's amazement when they realize that the lambs which the Hebrew slaves in Egypt sacrificed in order to put the blood on the doorposts was representative of Jesus' blood (John 1:29).

THE PASSOVER

God spoke to Moses and Aaron issuing several details for the congregation to observe prior to the Passover event. These details are listed in Exodus 12, and they are all symbolic of the future sacrifice of Jesus on the Cross (Jesus as the fulfillment in **bold**):

1) They were to get a male lamb of the first year – Exodus 12:5 **(John 1:29)**
2) The lamb had to be without blemish – Exodus 12:5 **(1 Peter 1:19)**
3) They had to examine the lamb on the 10th of Nisan (March-April) – Exodus 12:3 **(Luke 23:14)**
4) They killed (sacrificed) the lamb on the 14th of Nisan – Exodus 12:6 **(John 19:14-16)**
5) The lamb's blood would cause the judgment of God to "Passover" – Exodus 12:13 **(Romans 5:8, 9)**
6) They were to roast the lamb, and whatever was not eaten was to be burnt with fire – Exodus 12:10 **(Hebrews 13:11, 12)**
7) They were to eat unleavened bread (leaven is a symbol of sin) for 7 days from the 15th – 21st of Nisan – Exodus 12:18, 19 **(1 Corinthians 5:7, 8; John 6:51)**
8) They were not allowed to break any of the bones of the lamb – Exodus 12:46 **(John 19:31, 33; Psalms 34:20)**

In point five (5) above, the lamb's blood on the doorposts of the Hebrew slaves would cause the judgment of God to "pass over" those people inside (Exodus 12:13). Romans 5:8, 9 is the fulfillment of the Passover in which Jesus' blood from the Cross justified us from the wrath of God. God's judgment of sin will "pass over" us because we are covered by the blood of Jesus Christ.

THE REVELATION

I was reviewing this section of the Bible study when a particular section of verse 8 grabbed my attention, "In that, while we were yet sinners, Christ died for us." The Holy Spirit moved me to ponder the meaning of that and to personalize it. I began to consider Jesus dying on the Cross with the sole purpose of paying the penalty of my sins. Suddenly, the "while we were yet sinners" phrase caused me to visualize Jesus suffering excruciating pain while watching me in my rebellion of sin.

The weight of my sin increased exponentially, and my heart broke. I had looked back in time and I saw Jesus on the Cross gazing at me saying, "Robert, I love you so much that even though you are rebelling against me now, I will die for you." My love for Jesus was intensely amplified. I previously had a serious appreciation for the sacrifice Jesus paid for my sin, but this was a moment my words cannot caption. All I can say is that it became extraordinarily personal and immensely real. Feelings of disgust for my sin rose in proportionate levels to the rise of my love and appreciation for Jesus.

I invite you to read today's verses with the same context and instruction I received. Personalize the purpose of the sacrifice of Jesus on the Cross for your sins. Let the Holy Spirit speak to you as you envision Jesus performing the greatest act of love specifically for you. Realize the magnitude of God's love necessary to die for our behalf even though we were in rebellion to His will and purpose. God's amazing love for you is able to heal all things and release you from all strong holds.

Day 32

Psalm 103:12 - As far as the east is from the west, so far hath He removed our transgressions from us.

WE LEARNED IN Genesis 3:1 (Day 10) that Satan was the most cunning creature of any which God had made. The Devil has countless schemes to hinder a person's walk with God and to affect their ability to share a good testimony with others. The majority of his techniques are calculated to go undetected or to be ignored so we do not see his fingerprints on them. Today's verse is one that offers us a defense to a frequent and fertile tactic of his—guilt.

I have encountered scores of people who were thwarted from hearing God's will for them because of the weight of their guilt. Satan uses guilt to produce shame designed to cause a person to avoid God, His Word, and His people. It is a condemning act with the aim of producing abandonment of God's path and total capitulation of seeking God whatsoever. The deviousness of this ploy is that Satan disguises this guilt to be interpreted as if it is coming from God rather than Satan himself.

CARDINAL DIRECTION FACTS

Psalm 103:12 tells us that our sins have been removed from us "as far as the east is from the west." It is extremely significant that the Holy Spirit chose east and west over north and south. In the latter instance, the north and south meet twice at the two poles. For instance, each step you travel north brings you a step closer to where north and south intersect. Once you reach the North Pole, your next step is south.

What you may not have considered is that the east and west boundaries never intersect. If you hopped on a plane and spent a day flying westward all the way around the globe, you would not get an inch closer to east. The spiritual truth conveyed here is that God separates our sins from us in the same manner as the east is from the west. We can never reach them no matter which direction we choose. Once God forgives us, He removes that sin forever. He doesn't parade them in front of us, nor does He allow the weight of guilt to burden us.

A FRIENDLY BROKER

Early in my return to God, I was burdened with guilt over actions in my past. It seemed like the more I pursued God, the guiltier I felt. I was under assault from Satan, and it was working. I felt terribly discouraged in my walk, and I wasn't experiencing God's joy and peace (Galatians 5:22). I instinctively shunned all communication with God like prayer, Bible reading, and fellowship with believers. I discarded all the spiritual tools of assistance God makes readily available to all of us.

I was working in my role as a real estate developer, and I was chatting via email with a wonderful broker named Nyoka Johnston. I had communicated my circumstances which led to my return to God. In that email, I shared with her that I was feeling incredible guilt. She responded back with our verse today, and

I will always remember how quickly and noticeably my burden departed. The vacuum of guilt's departure was filled with the joy and peace I had been yearning for.

Satan wants to affect your walk with God in any way possible. He will even try to blur God's conviction into condemnation. The Bible reveals to us that God does not condemn those who are in Jesus (Romans 8:1; John 3:17), but rather God reveals our faults to us for correction. If ever you recognize the guilt of repented sins upon yourself, speak aloud our verse today, and let God's Word defeat Satan's effort.

Day 33

Luke 6:46 - And why call ye me, Lord, Lord, and do not the things which I say?

JUST TWO DAYS ago, I took my oldest daughter to the orthodontist to get braces installed. Sydney has an incredibly small mouth, and many of her teeth have no room to come down. For that reason, she previously had to go to an oral surgeon to have six teeth removed—four wisdom teeth, one permanent tooth, and one impacted baby tooth. Needless to say, Sydney loathes anybody associated with a dentist.

Her elevated anxiety was manifested during the orthodontist visit by an uncontrollable and continuous flow of tears. I had prepared her all week leading up to this occasion with constant reassurance that there would not be any pain associated with the procedure of putting on braces, but she still succumbed to the influence of her fears. I was holding her hand while she inconsolably cried, and I began to feel frustrated because she didn't trust me that everything would be okay. I was saddened and irritated as I watched my daughter reacting fearfully to every tool the orthodontist introduced to her.

GOD SPEAKS TO ME

I wanted desperately for Sydney to not experience any unnecessary distress and trepidation. I reasoned that if she would have only trusted me, she would have had a much shorter and better experience. It was at this moment that God spoke to me by letting me know that His heart is breaking for His children like my heart was breaking for Sydney. So many of His sons and daughters are dealing with unnecessary dismay and apprehension because they do not trust what their Father has said.

Today's verse validates what I was hearing from God. In our verse, Jesus questions the contradiction of people calling Him "Lord, Lord" and not doing what He says. Luke 6:46 captions a prevalent problem which exists now within the churches across the globe, as well as for centuries past: people professing their faith in God in words only. These people do not have any testimony to share because they have not responded to the convictions from the Holy Spirit, nor have they yielded to any instruction in the Bible. They do not experience the blessings and fruition of the many precious promises of God in their lives.

ABSOLUTE LOVE

I would have done anything possible to alleviate Sydney's panic and torment at the orthodontist's office. Although my love for my daughters is absolute, deep, and sincere, it cannot compare to God's love for us (John 15:13). In addition to dying for us, He has spoken extensively on all matters of life so we can inherit an abundantly peaceful life (Psalm 37:11). If we truly make Jesus "Lord," we will walk according to His Word, we will flee the worldly desires when warned, and we will search daily for God's will in our lives.

Our Father in heaven yearns for each of us to trust in Him completely. He has purposed an abundant life for each of us in

His divine will, and only He is absolutely capable to navigate our paths perfectly. He alone is able to see each and every hidden pitfall in this sinful world planted there by Satan to entrap us. He is readily waiting for each and every one of us with a loving heart saying, "Trust Me!"

Are you ready to truly make Jesus Lord over ALL your life? If you look closely at your walk with God, can you see where you have been putting your will for your life over God's will for your life? If so, take this moment to confess that realization to God and give Him the reigns now. Surrender the vulnerable self-will for the all-powerful God's will.

Day 34

1 John 4:8 - He that loveth not knoweth not God; for God is love.

1 JOHN 4:8 is a simple little verse which sums up the nature of God—"God is love." It also reasons that if you do not love others, then you do not have an understanding of God. The implication is that the more we know of God, the more our love will grow for others.

Some years ago, God put it on my heart to demonstrate to my wife and daughters the value and importance I held for my relationship with Him. I wanted to lead my family to God in an additional manner to taking them to church. That conviction turned into a devotional every evening at 8:30. We gather on the floor around our coffee table to memorize a weekly verse, to read a chapter out of the Bible, to sing a song, and to pray for someone else.

It wasn't too long afterwards, that today's verse became our memory verse, and because of its significance, we incorporated a new component to our devotion. We each take a turn to tell everybody in the circle that we love them. This new addition was a big hit with the little kids. Since we often had neighbor children participating with us during devotion there were many moments of giggling and laughter. The fascinating observation was the ease at which troubled kids in the neighborhood transformed from embarrassing hesitation to full blown enthusiasm! We were created by God to love one another, and children respond dutifully (Luke 18:17).

AGAPE LOVE

Americans in general have an unfortunate distortion in their understanding of love. It has become the cultural norm in our society to move from relationship to relationship. People excuse this with statements like "I just fell out of love with him," "she is not the same person I married back then," or "we just ended up going in different directions." Our idea of love is defectively selfish and disheartening.

In our passage today, the word "love" is the translation of the Greek word *agape*. In our effort to comprehend the meaning of this love, we need to examine the Greek definition:

> **Agape** – Agape love is a <u>pure commitment</u> of love from the one who loves, and it requires no action or response from the target of the love. It does not change, nor is it conditional.

Love is not an emotional feeling that we catch or fall into; love is a commitment that we make and keep. We are instructed throughout the Bible to love each other in the same standard which God loves us.

GOD'S UNCONDITIONAL LOVE

1 Corinthians 13 is commonly referred to as the Love Chapter. In the thirteen verses of this chapter, agape is listed nine times, and it is the sole emphasis of the topic. Since our verse today tells us that God is agape, I thought it relevant to list what 1 Corinthians says about agape:

- Agape is patient
- Agape is kind
- Agape doesn't envy
- Agape doesn't boast
- Agape is not arrogant or rude
- Agape is not selfish
- Agape is not irritable or resentful
- Agape doesn't like wrongdoing
- Agape rejoices in the truth
- Agape bears all things
- Agape believes all things
- Agape is hopeful
- Agape is enduring
- Agape never fails
- Agape never ends

Although God's salvation is conditioned upon our willingness to accept His free gift, His love for us is unconditional. It is the reason that God sent His Son, Jesus Christ, to die on the Cross (John 3:16—"agape love"). It is the "agape love" which Jesus declared was above any other type of love (John 15:13). It is "agape love" which husbands are to love their wives (Colossians 3:19), and it is "agape love" which we are commanded to have for each other (John 13:34).

In light of what agape love means, I encourage you to reflect on the love you have for others. Is your love conditioned upon how you are treated or regarded? Do you withdraw or alter your love upon conflict, insult, or displeasure? Divorce rates in America broadcast that we do not have agape love in our marriages. Church attendance decline indicates that agape love is missing in many of them. There is an enormous need within the body of Christ to transform our perception of love into His agape love. Will you answer His call to agape love?

Day 35

> Revelation 12:11 - And they overcame him by the blood of the Lamb, and by the word of their testimony; and they loved not their lives unto the death.

WE ARE COMPLETING our fifth and final full week of our forty-day venture together, and I am excited to share with you several amazing truths which the Holy Spirit has revealed to me in today's verse.

Revelation 12:11 is the basis of Jeremy Camp's hit song "*Overcome*," which speaks about the power of God available to all believers of Jesus Christ. It is power to overcome Satan and his tactics designed to kill, steal, and destroy. Here, God is giving us the two components for overcoming Satan—the blood of Jesus and our testimony.

BLOOD OF THE LAMB

The blood of the Lamb is the key issue for the whole world. Only the blood of Jesus saves us from the judgment of God. There is no other way to obtain eternal life than through Jesus' blood

(John 14:6; Acts 4:12). God repeatedly reveals that He is just and requiring of judgment upon all sin (Deuteronomy 32:4; Isaiah 45:21). Jesus humbled Himself by becoming man and entered His creation in order to die in our place to satisfy God's verdict of death for sin (Romans 6:23; Genesis 2:17).

Unfortunately, there are many people who look upon their minister as the focus of their worship. They hear God's Word being spoken, but they associate His Words with the person speaking them instead of God. They marvel at the perceived godliness of the preacher in lieu of having a personal relationship with the living God. They think their pastor walks on water instead of being in awe of the One who really did walk on water. Ministry leaders must not allow themselves to fill that role, but rather always pointing those admirations to Jesus.

I was mentoring a man out of prison, and he called me desperate about his truck not working. For someone at a halfway house, transportation to work is indispensable and funds for repairs are utterly lacking. I asked him to pray with me about the vehicle, and I recall being inspired not to communicate my willingness to help him financially with the repair. Afterwards, he diagnosed the starter as the malfunctioning part, and I took him to a nearby AutoZone store where his diagnosis was confirmed.

It was this next moment in which this man saw God do a miracle for him and his faith was increased. In consternation of hearing the clerk give him the unattainable cost for a replacement part, he became flabbergasted to learn that his brother had previously installed the starter on his truck while he was in prison, and AutoZone had a warranty on it. Instead of this man looking at me in solving his problem, he saw God do it!

NOW HE HAS A TESTIMONY

God had shown me that I can interfere with His plan by trying to act on His behalf. In the time since then, He has given me such clarity on this point. He speaks to me about helping people when able, and pointing others to Him with absolute confidence that God will be there for them (Hebrews 13:6).

This man now has a testimony about how he saw God act in his life. He has since experienced many more occasions where God directly intervened on his behalf in life. He has become an inspiring leader in Celebrate Recovery (a Christ-centered recovery program), and he has spoken publicly about all that God has done in him. I have seen the fruit from this man sharing how the blood of Jesus has saved him and testifying how God has provided and helped him to a new and better life.

We are called to share with others what God has done for us. We are to tell people about His love, provision, and protection for us. Have you experienced God's blessing in your life? If so, then your story is greatly important for others to overcome Satan. Your testimony of God's change in your life is a significant event in helping others. Keep it simple—Jesus died for your sins ("blood of the Lamb") and your "testimony" about how He has impacted your new life.

Day 36

Psalm 86:15 - But thou, O Lord, art a God full of compassion, and gracious, longsuffering, and plenteous in mercy and truth.

AS WE APPROACH the culmination of this study, I thought it beneficial to spend another day captivating the attributes of God. I have found it necessary in my life to revisit this verse to be reminded about His nature of sympathy and forgiveness for me.

Notice how this verse reinforces the forgiving nature of God; He is "full of compassion." God never runs out of compassion for you and me. In a cold and callous world that doesn't care whether you live or die, I find it tremendously comforting that I cannot exhaust His empathy for me. He is full of compassion for you as well.

God is gracious. The great evangelist and writer Hal Lindsey defines grace by its acronym—**G**od's **R**iches **A**t **C**hrist's **E**xpense. Where mercy is defined as not getting what we deserved, grace is defined as getting what we don't deserve. You and I did not deserve to have the Holy Son of God come into His creation and die an excruciating death for our sins, but that is the prime demonstration of God's grace for us. I am so thankful that God is gracious, and blesses me with things that I do not deserve. Are you?

God is longsuffering (patient). I am a severely flawed individual, and nowhere does this fact show up more than my lack of patience. I am so thankful that God does not possess my same shortfall. He is extraordinarily patient with you and me, waiting compassionately for His children. I am in awe of how patient God was in waiting for me to make Him Lord over all of my life. Did you require God's patience as well? Are you in need of it still?

God is overflowing with mercy. He has so much mercy for us that He can hardly contain it. As a minister to men in jail and prison, I have seen God's attribute of mercy literally bring hardened men to weep. Mercy has an amazing effect on people that cannot be accomplished through any other means. In my own walk with God, I have needed to approach Him with an appeal for His mercy. I am so thankful that He has an ample amount to give me. Do you need God's mercy? Are you thankful that He has a lot of it?

God is plenteous in truth. This attribute is probably the one which is most often disregarded by believers, but it is a characteristic loaded with power to affect our lives. People can spend an entire lifetime clouded in the lie of the world and suffering under the weight of its sinfulness. Even Christians can succumb to the deceptions of Satan when their eyes are taken away from God. God will reveal truth to all areas of our lives: truth about decisions that need to be made, truth about changes which need to be made, truth about concealed adversaries, truth about harmful institutions and traditions, and truth about His love and power for us. I marvel at the truth which He has already revealed to me. Do you desire to know His truth?

THE MOTIVATION

Just a couple of days ago, I wrote to you about an experience I underwent with my oldest daughter at the orthodontist. Sydney has a learning disability which causes her to have great difficulty with many things others take for granted. One of those difficulties is a paralyzing anxiety of all the foreign objects which the orthodontist attached to her teeth. In my efforts to teach her to floss with her new braces, I lost my temper with her constant capitulation to her fear. I responded by yelling at her.

I soon realized my error, and I asked for her forgiveness. We prayed together as I asked for God's forgiveness as well. I felt a resolute shame that I could not shake. I was under attack from Satan (Revelation 12:10), and I was succumbing to it. That is when God led me to this verse which I spoke out loud. I said, "I won't believe your lies Satan. God is full of compassion and mercy for me, and He is not casting me off because of my failure. God is patient with me and He has much grace for me, so you should flee from me." This attack on me ceased immediately, and my shame fled as well.

Have you felt Satan's attack on you in a similar manner? If so, keep this verse close to your heart and proclaim it aloud in a similar time of trouble.

Day 37

Job 33:14 - For God speaketh once, yea twice, yet man perceiveth it not.

I OFTEN GET opportunities within this ministry to visit with young men who recently came to know God. In these occasions, I will frequently get asked a specific question, "How do you hear God?"

That question is one that I used to ask of others, and it was something that I desired immensely to know. I was so engrossed in searching for clarity from God that I initiated a Prayer & Fast retreat with the sole purpose of hearing from God. I tasked myself with an assignment to prepare and lead the group in a Bible study on hearing the Holy Spirit, and today's verse was a key component.

GOD IS TALKING TO US ALL THE TIME

The verse tells us that God is speaking to us many times in various ways, but we are not observing it. God communicates with us in a spiritual manner, and we have been restricted to listening in a natural manner (1 Corinthians 2:14; Romans 8:16). With that being stated, we should realize that God is talking to us, and we are the ones who are hindering the communication because we haven't been listening spiritually for Him.

The number one way God speaks to us is with the Bible. All other means of hearing from God should be filtered through the Bible first for affirmation of God's written Word. Paul distinguished the Bereans as being more noble than the Thessalonians because they searched the scriptures daily to prove true what they heard from others (Acts 17:11).

When I returned to God, the first thing that I did was open my Bible with an intention of hearing God speak to me. On countless occasions, I have experienced God speaking directly to me through His Word; and on countless occasions I have marveled how specific and responsive He was to me. Even now, I often find myself amazed at how directly God's Word will speak to a specific situation in my life. Although it is a verse that I have read many times, its relevance to a current circumstance I am going through makes it seem like it was inserted in the Bible that day specifically for me.

I have heard many men complain about not hearing from God only to learn that they never open their Bible. Jeremiah 29:13 tells us that we will find God if we will seek Him with all our heart. How can we search God with all our heart without reading His Word? The answer is obvious and convicting. If we want to hear from God, we need to consume His Word, not just accomplish a reading assignment.

God speaks to me through many different ways. I hear from Him through pastors, preachers, teachers, music, friends, events and nature, just to name a few. All those mediums require me to first have an obedient heart that is searching to hear from God. I must initiate a readiness to hear from God by praying and submitting myself to His will. I must approach God with a submissive spirit to yield to His authority over my life.

God has answered my prayers seeking guidance in decision-making by overwhelming me with an unexplainable peace towards a particular choice. I have heard answers from God to specific prayer petitions by thoughts and impressions (Day 6 / Proverbs 16:3), and I have heard distinctly from God during prayer fasts with such clarity and closeness that is hard for me to describe the intensity of His presence.

ARE YOU READY TO HEAR GOD

God is speaking to you all the time; God is speaking to you right now. Are you eager to hear from Him? If so, then take specific actions to hear Him:

1) Pray to God right now and ask Him to help you hear from Him,
2) Prepare your heart by elevating the desire to hear from Him,
3) Open your Bible each day with an anticipation that God will speak to you through His Word,
4) Expect to hear back from God—listen for Him,
5) Search for His peace on decisions which need to be made,
6) Finally, acknowledge Him, thank Him, and glorify Him when He answers you.

Day 38

1 Timothy 1:5 (NKJV) - Now the purpose of the commandment is love from a pure heart, from a good conscience, and from sincere faith,

TODAY'S VERSE CONTAINS a word within it that has risen to such prominence for me personally when studying God's Word—purpose. I was reading Richard D. Phillips' book, *The Masculine Mandate: God's Calling to Men*, and I was quite intrigued by how he focused on the purpose of why God created man, the purpose of why God created woman, the purpose of marriage, and the purpose of the curses from God.

We are informed in this verse that the purpose of God's commandments is love (agape). A lawyer once asked Jesus which is the greatest commandment. Jesus replied that the greatest commandment is to love God with all our heart, soul, and mind (Matthew 22:37-38). He then tells us the next greatest commandment is to love others like we love ourselves (v. 39). Jesus then tells the lawyer that all the law and the prophets hang on those two commandments to love God and each other. The law and prophets would represent the whole Bible. The purpose of the Bible is so that we will love (agape) God and each other!

LOVE DEMONSTRATED AT WAL-MART

Several years ago, God was dealing with me about this subject. He was impressing upon me a desire to see other people like He does, and more importantly, to love other people like He loves them. This was on my mind one day walking into Wal-Mart when I noticed this individual in front of me. This person instantly generated in me feelings of repugnance. Everything about this person was objectionable to me: the look, the clothes, the walk, the chomping of gum, and even the hair.

I remember saying a quick prayer asking God to help me see this particular individual like He does. I followed (not stalking) this person to the back of the store, and before I was half-way there, the repulsion which I had previously felt turned into compassion. I was experiencing genuine sympathy as I realized that many of the things I initially found offensive were a result of a poor self-esteem in this person. I realized that this poor self-image was probably caused by a lack of a relationship with a loving God. I began to wonder what the relationship with the parents was like and whether or not there was a lack of love there. In the matter of thirty seconds, I was transformed to feel great empathy which overwhelmed me. God had made His point to me!

GOD'S PURPOSE FOR THE BIBLE

1 Timothy 1:5 reveals that God's purpose for giving us the Bible is so that we will have a love for Him and others. He wants us to have an agape love like His agape love for us. He wants us to become more like Jesus, and He is the One who does the work in us if we will allow it (Philippians 1:6).

When we read the Bible, we need to remember the purpose God gave us. If we will do that, we will be more discerning to the convictions of God as we analyze His commandments in our own lives. We will be expecting to hear the Holy Spirit addressing the pureness of our hearts. Our decisions and actions will all fall under an act of love for God and others.

Will you continue to allow God to do His full work in you? Are you ready to let God create a pure heart in you which will pour out His love for others? This is a lifelong process which we can hinder at any time with complacency or apathy. We must be diligent every day to allow God's work to be done in our lives so that we can be equipped with the most powerful weapon to overcome sin and death—pure love!

Day 39

> **Revelation 3:15-16 - I know thy works, that thou art neither cold nor hot: I would thou wert cold or hot.**
>
> **So then because thou art lukewarm, and neither cold nor hot, I will spue thee out of my mouth.**

I WAS IN the gym yesterday contemplating the many logistics for publishing and marketing this book when God led me to think about people asking me the why question—"Why did you write this book?" I began to fashion my answer beyond the actuality of God instructing me to do it. I thought about the many promptings of God to compose my testimonies reflecting God's Word being fulfilled in my life. It became very obvious to me that I could not tell my own testimony without including Revelation 3:15-16.

Our verses come from a letter Jesus dictates to the Church of Laodicea in which He rebukes them for being neither cold nor hot. He is implying that their love and faith in God is so-so. They can take church or leave it. They are not opposed to God on one hand, but they are not on fire for Him on the other hand. Jesus' response to their apathy was to vomit ("spue") them out of His mouth. Jesus voices His disgust by saying He would prefer that they would be callous to God rather than to be "lukewarm."

JESUS' WORDS CUT ME TO THE BONE

During the portion of my life when I was hiding from God, I would occasionally frequent church (Easter, Christmas, funeral, a girlfriend takes me, guilt complex from mom or dad, etc.), and Revelation 3:15-16 would seem to come up. Jesus' Words seemed to speak directly to me. I believed in God; I was saved, but I was not living for Him. I was living in a lifestyle of deliberate sin, and I didn't want to hear His conviction. I didn't renounce God, but He didn't have any real significance in my life. I was "lukewarm."

Throughout this fifteen-year deviation from God, I would sporadically be intrigued to read Revelation. Whenever I reached these verses, I would intentionally skip them so as to avert the realization that Jesus wanted to vomit me out of His mouth. I was desperate to avoid facing the truth of my life choices and how they were received by God.

THE PRODIGAL SON RETURNS

Thank God that I finally came to a point where I surrendered my whole life to Him. Soon afterwards, my new commitment to read the Bible led me to these verses again, and previous feelings of shame and regret were revisited. I heard Jesus' conviction again, but on this occasion I followed His instruction to repent (v. 19). All the negative feelings and guilt were vanquished by His grace and love. I no longer caused Jesus to want to *"spue"* me out of His mouth; I was no longer lukewarm!

In my experience in ministry, I have seen several instances where people who were once on fire for God became complacent. God brought them out of their desperate situation, and they seemed to forget about Him. They enjoy the blessing of God, but they do not want to have a relationship with the One who blessed them. They profess a faith in God, but they don't have time for Him.

There is a real spiritual danger to some people in becoming comfortable in their faith. They can be very indifferent to God's Word, His Will, and His conviction when God removes the desperation that brought them to Him. They can get satisfied with the limited relationship that they have with God at that specific moment and spend the rest of their lives idle and distant from the intimate relationship which God desires for them.

Be wary of the warning in this letter to the Church of Laodicea and guard against apathy and indifference. Treasure your relationship with Jesus Christ by always seeking to draw closer to Him. Be deliberate in pursuing His will for your life and strive to know Him better. Fan the flames of love that God birthed in you when you came to His Cross by being thankful to Him every day.

Day 40

1 John 5:4 - For whatsoever is born of God overcometh the world: and this is the victory that overcometh the world, even our faith.

WE HAVE REACHED our destination of a forty-day walk through God's Word in search for His will in our lives. I'm so thrilled for the fulfillment of the commitment you made at the beginning of this book, and I pray that your desire for God's Word was stimulated through it.

When I embarked on writing this book, I had purposed to save this verse for the last day. It is a verse whose significance only grows deeper with spiritual maturity. This verse is ideal for amplifying what you have hopefully experienced numerous times over the past five and a half weeks—achieving victories over the world through God's Word.

OVERCOMER

This inspiring verse informs us that we, believers in Jesus Christ, have a destiny to overcome the world. This promise applies to us individually, and is not limited to a specific group or community of believers. You will have individual victories over the destructive nature of the sinful world. You will have victories over addictions, victories over bitterness, victories over materialism, victories over vanity, and victories over any other trap which Satan uses to steal, kill, and destroy (John 10:10 / Day 2).

Victories are not automatic just because someone believes in Jesus. We are instructed that we have a role to play in order to achieve those victories, and here lies the secret—*faith!* We must have faith in order to have victory over the world. Faith in what? Faith in God's Word. We need to have faith believing that if we do what God instructs us to do; we will be blessed in the manner in which He promises. Likewise, we need to have faith in avoiding the allures and enticements of worldly things in which God tells us are harmful to us.

GOD'S PURPOSE FOR US

I am hopeful that you have already experienced this truth many times through this forty-day journey. This verse is encouraging the believer to pursue one's life with an expectation that victories over all the snares of the world are absolutely attainable. We can achieve the abundant life promised by Jesus when we walk in faith. We have a free will to choose to live by faith, or to live by our own will and understanding. Which one will you choose to live by?

God wants a personal relationship with you. He wants to walk with you as He did with Adam and Eve in the Garden of Eden. He has an infinite love for you which is beyond our ability to comprehend. Because of His love for you, He wants to guide your life to fulfill His specific calling for you. If you will trust Him, you will live a life full of love, joy, and peace (Galatians 5).

It is my prayer for you that your desire for God will grow daily. I pray that you will experience God's blessings to the fullest. I pray that your **new life** will be fruitful and full of joy. I pray that your faith will continue to be strengthened and your inheritance to be realized.

Congratulations on completing this study, and may God bless you and your family!

CPSIA information can be obtained
at www.ICGtesting.com
Printed in the USA
BVHW032135240220
573228BV00001B/19